# Conversations with Flannery O'Connor

## Literary Conversations Series

*Peggy Whitman Prenshaw*
*General Editor*

# Conversations
# with Flannery O'Connor

*Edited by*
*Rosemary M. Magee*

University Press of Mississippi
Jackson and London

**Books by Flannery O'Connor**

*Wise Blood.* New York: Harcourt, Brace and Co., 1952.

*A Good Man Is Hard to Find.* New York: Harcourt, Brace and Co., 1955.

*The Violent Bear It Away.* New York: Farrar, Straus and Cudahy, 1960.

*Everything That Rises Must Converge.* New York: Farrar, Straus and Giroux, 1965.

*Mystery and Manners: The Occasional Prose of Flannery O'Connor.* Edited by Sally and Robert Fitzgerald. New York: Farrar, Straus and Giroux, 1969.

*The Complete Stories of Flannery O'Connor.* New York: Farrar, Straus and Giroux, 1971.

*The Habit of Being: Letters of Flannery O'Connor.* Edited by Sally Fitzgerald. New York: Farrar, Straus and Giroux, 1979.

*The Presence of Grace and Other Book Reviews by Flannery O'Connor.* Compiled by Leo Zuber and edited by Carter Martin. Athens, Georgia: University of Georgia Press, 1983.

Copyright © 1987 by the University Press of Mississippi
All rights reserved
Manufactured in the United States of America
90  89  88  87    4  3  2  1

Photo © Joe McTyre/Atlanta Constitution

The paper in this book meets the guidelines for permanence and durability
of the Committee on Production Guidelines for Book Longevity
of the Council on Library Resources.

**Library of Congress Cataloging-in-Publication Data**

O'Connor, Flannery.
    Conversations with Flannery O'Connor.

    (Literary conversations series)
    Includes index.
    1. O'Connor, Flannery—Interviews.   2. Authors.
American—20th century—Interviews.   I. Magee,
Rosemary M.   II. Title.   III. Series.
PS3565.C57Z464   1987          813'.54          86-22381
ISBN 0-87805-264-X
ISBN 0-87805-265-8 (pbk.)

British Library Cataloguing in Publication data is available.

# Contents

# Introduction

⌐

"At interviews," Flannery O'Connor wrote to her friend Cecil Dawkins, "I always feel like a dry cow being milked. There is no telling what they will get out of you. . . . If you do manage to say anything that makes sense, they put down the opposite."[1] Such anxieties might lead to the conclusion that O'Connor's interviews add little to an understanding of her fiction and her character. But the interviews themselves—both as separate entities and even more as a collection—indicate otherwise. There are about a dozen formal interviews and an assortment of other articles based on conversations published in an unusual array of periodicals. Characterized by terse, but careful and thoughtful replies, they exhibit remarkable consistency and coherency with O'Connor's other published works. At the same time they reveal new aspects of this complex southern writer.

A native of a region blessed with what she named the "storytelling habit," Flannery O'Connor won acclaim for her ability to write stories of extraordinary depth and subtle detail. Through narrative O'Connor revealed her vision of the world. In addition to those that she told, many stories have now been told *about* her and her fiction in a variety of forms. Her collected letters display the network of her human relations; her book reviews and marginal comments in her library provide her response to other works of the imagination, criticism, and philosophy. In her lectures and essays she consciously strove to make sense of her own fiction and the processes of creating. Many reminiscences of her demonstrate her influence on a wide community of friends and scholars. A forthcoming biography by Sally Fitzgerald promises to capture the texture of her life; criticism of her

1. *The Habit of Being: Letters of Flannery O'Connor*, ed. Sally Fitzgerald (New York: Farrar, Straus and Giroux, 1979), p. 306. Letter dated 9 December 1958. Further references to the collected letters will be cited within text in the following manner: (Date—*HB*, p. _____).

fiction shows her place in the literary world. Her interviews reveal her attitudes and manner of speech and thought. They also display her quick wit, incisive mind, and gracious style. The collected interviews, then, provide an additional glimpse of her that nonetheless meshes with what is already known. They too tell a story.

Despite a large number of friends and a certain proclivity toward conversation and storytelling, O'Connor's responses to direct questions are frequently laconic or terse. The interviewer asks a question, and O'Connor replies with an obvious and short (though still polite) answer. Often her interviewers seem thrown off balance by her manner and style, yet they consistently describe her as friendly, polite, and candid. Granville Hicks, in his meeting with her in 1962, found her to be "a pleasant, poised, quiet young woman, rather inscrutable . . . but instantly likable. She talks well, answering questions concisely and without the least hesitation, and I have no doubt that she is a woman who knows her own mind."[2] Joel Wells described her as "candid" but also "graciously tolerant" of questions. Another interviewer, Margaret Turner, stated her assessment succinctly: "She's not prone to indulge in idle chatter." In almost every instance O'Connor charmed her interviewers, although they were frequently puzzled by her sometimes sardonic sense of humor. Like any good storyteller, she had certain favorite tales which she could not resist repeating. When she was a child (reported in different interviews at age five, six, or eleven) she owned a chicken that became known for its ability to walk backwards. Pathé News traveled to Milledgeville to capture on film this unusual bird and its young owner. O'Connor liked to conclude the telling of the story in this way: "Since that big event my life has been an anti-climax." She enjoyed mocking herself as well as others.

Taken together, these interviews add a new dimension to an appreciation of O'Connor and, as a result, to an understanding of her fiction. They demonstrate in many different times and places her interactions with others and her responses to direct questions about her work; they also exhibit interviewers' opinions of her and their

2. "A Writer at Home with her Heritage," interview with Granville Hicks in *Saturday Review*, 45 (12 May 1962), 22. Further references to interviews will indicate the interviewer, the journal in which it appeared, or the place where it was conducted.

responses to her. They place O'Connor within a literary and historical and social framework. What becomes clearer than anywhere else in the works by and about O'Connor is the remarkable clarity of her beliefs as well as her self-consciousness and deliberateness as an artist. In all of the interviews she talks with ease about her ideas and beliefs; in only a few, however, does she speak freely about her own fiction or about her own personal or religious experiences. Yet despite her best efforts to maintain some privacy, the interviews as a collection succeed in telling a good bit about her as a person—her habits and feelings as well as her ideas. She exhibits a certain constancy and congruency in fiction, letters, reviews, and interviews which belie her unsophisticated manner. Her modest demeanor and frequently self-deprecating humor are in sharp contrast to her precise and careful responses to questions. Throughout the interviews, as in all her published work, an unchanging yet dynamic vision of life emerges.

O'Connor's letters often give her own impressions of an interview: her expectations beforehand, her perception of how it proceeded, and finally her response to the published version. The interviews, then, offer a useful contrast *and* complement to her letters, in which she expresses her private thoughts to friends or trusted correspondents. The interviews—along with her essays and lectures, and perhaps reaching a wider audience than either during her lifetime—forged her public identity. Unlike her letters, which were rarely intended for more than one person, they were granted with the full knowledge that they would be published. Her thoughts in both letters and interviews are presented with careful reflection and precision, even when delivered extemporaneously. She gives insight into the creative process, but she does not attempt to explain her fiction. She always presumed that literary texts could and would stand on their own. She did, however, set out to elucidate the beliefs which empowered her fiction. Interestingly, after those interviews in which she sounds most self-assured, she writes letters to her friends expressing her fears of her own inarticulateness. Like most authors, she dreaded the thought of being misquoted; perhaps more than most she loathed the possibility of being misrepresented. O'Connor was fully aware of the fact that her ideas were unusual, complex, and carefully constructed; she presented them in an exact manner. She did not trust her interviewers to rephrase them nor the subsequent audience of readers to make sense of reformulated versions.

For O'Connor, the fabric of her life and her theology was interwoven with her fiction. When one of her interviewers, Joel Wells, asked her about the meaning of her second novel, *The Violent Bear It Away*, she replied, "It's a matter of vocation." For her it was a story about choice for the young Tarwater; he could choose the religious vocation of his fanatical but righteous great-uncle or the rational and secular path of his uncle. In all human life, she argued, there is this choice of vocation. O'Connor strongly believed that she had been called to offer in fiction her own vision of life. But her vocation did not end there. Despite giving the impression at times that she was a recluse and that she disliked intrusions, she felt compelled to explain her beliefs and ideas in essays, lectures, and interviews. There can be no question about the importance to her of the vocation of a writer. She was called to write about what she saw; and for those who could not comprehend it in ordinary language she was able to use the devices—the symbols, metaphors, and exaggerations—permitted in fiction. The importance of vocation in her fiction reveals its importance in her own life. On this level, she has much in common with Hazel Motes and the younger as well as the elder Tarwater. Like them, she responded to a call and was, in a sense, driven by it.

In interviews O'Connor was consistently questioned about the literature and social conditions of the South. Reluctant to generalize about either, she did her best to counteract many prevailing national opinions about both. She defended the South, but not by resorting to simple chauvinistic or romanticized platitudes about the region, a predictable response of many southerners to criticism. Rather, she argued that the traditions of storytelling and the presence of a Biblical reality, along with prevailing patterns of interactions and social arrangments ("manners"), provided an interesting and cohesive culture—despite its many complications and contradictions—for the southerner in general and for the southern writer in particular. She believed that, unlike other regions of the country, the South had a sense of history and of place but that all of this was under assault by the processes of industrialization. She expressed concern about the loss of meaning and belief, about the demise of a sense of individuality and regional identity in a constantly changing universe where "everything is reduced to the same flat level" (*Vagabond*).

Violence in O'Connor's fiction, along with the assorted collection of deformities and the frequency of bizarre behavior, inspired many questions from interviewers. In response, she talked quite directly about the meaning and nature of the grotesque in literature and what it signified in her own fiction. Frequently accused of concentrating on the tawdry, ugly aspects of human nature and life, at Vanderbilt she readily replied, "I think it is easier to come out with something that is negative because it is just nearer fallen nature." She further maintained that fiction cannot be simply a vehicle for other ideas or religious beliefs: "You don't ever prove anything when you write a story." Fiction must have a dramatic integrity of its own; but she also believed, as she explained to Harvey Breit, that "a serious fiction writer describes an action only in order to reveal a mystery." For her, "The sense of mystery is apparent in all good fiction." (*Motley*). Despite the different ends of theology and literature, she managed to integrate them; she then added a strong dose of common sense. The results were fascinating fiction and compelling interviews.

When quizzed about her approach to writing, O'Connor was willing to explain that she wrote every morning for three hours, but she consistently cautioned that there is no magic formula. The writer writes because it is a necessity, a calling. In many ways, she explained to Joel Wells, serious writers are like the Old Testament prophets who dedicated themselves to the task of "recalling people to known but ignored truths." They must be able to see through the many levels of life and uncover the mystery that lurks there. For her, "In every story there is some minor revelation which, no matter how funny the story may be, gives us a hint of the unknown, of death" *(Esprit)*. She admitted to interviewer C. Ross Mullins, Jr., that she was preoccupied "with belief and with death and grace and the devil," and that she did not wish to circumvent the issues and problems posed by death: "I'm a born Catholic and death has always been brother to my imagination. I can't imagine a story that doesn't properly end in it or in its foreshadowings." The critical factor in good writing, she repeated over and over, is to keep going deeper; life is not simply what it appears to be; through fiction one may delve beneath the surface.

In her first interview of substance—taped for the television program "Galley Proof" and transcribed from that tape for this collection—Harvey Breit, an experienced if not expert interviewer, had difficulty eliciting lengthy responses from O'Connor. It is clear that they are both ill at ease. Breit seems unnerved by her concise and concrete answers; O'Connor seems put off by the verbose and urbane Breit. At times he answers his own questions. He is particularly disturbed when he asks O'Connor if she would like to summarize the remaining part of her story "The Life You Save May Be Your Own" after the first portion had just been dramatized; O'Connor quite simply refuses: "No, I certainly would not." She explained that the story could not be paraphrased or explained; it tells itself. Even at this early stage in her career she was clear about how she felt, what she would and would not do and what she believed.

Before the interview in a letter to Robie Macauley, O'Connor admitted to her fears: "I will probably not be able to think of anything to say to Mr. Harvey Breit but 'Huh?' and 'Ah dunno' (18 May 1855—HB, p. 81). Afterwards in a letter to close friends she confirmed that the experience had been "mildly ghastly" (10 June 1955—HB, p. 85). Despite the stilted interaction between Breit and O'Connor, the interview reveals a good bit about her. In particular, she emphasized the importance of a writer being located—artistically and emotionally, at least—in a region; she then stressed the importance of self-knowledge in order to overcome simplistic regionalism. One must be a part of the world yet in exile from it. With each successive interview, the precision of her articulation of her beliefs increased. This development had to do with her growing maturity as a writer, with her wider range of experience, and also with her efforts to control interviews carefully. She began to believe that unless she exerted her own will, she would be at the mercy of the interviewer.

The next year when O'Connor participated in a literary discussion at Emory University in Atlanta, she felt that she was misrepresented by Celestine Sibley, a popular writer for the Altanta papers. Although she was certainly given a sympathetic review by this sympathetic reporter, who declared her "the hit of the season," she was disturbed by the impression she might have left. The difficulty, she felt, was that she was expected to entertain and not to educate. Before the event, in a letter to her close friend "A," she compared the format to that of a zoo—with a different animal, or writer, coming to visit each week. To another friend she stated, "I am going to end my lecture on the note that it is as noble not to write as to" (31 January 1957—*HB*, p. 201). She did not wish to unleash on the world unskilled and uncommitted writers. Afterwards O'Connor wrote that she was dismayed by the review in the Atlanta newspaper; it left the mistaken impression, she felt, that she held the audience in contempt (21 February 1957—*HB*, p. 203). In a letter to Maryat Lee, once more describing the event, she disclosed her self-conscious inclination to respond to questions with "deathly stupid" remarks (24 February 1957—*HB*, p. 204). She feared that to audiences as well as to journalists and their readers she might appear to be mean-spirited and ignorant.

In 1958 O'Connor consented to answer questions submitted to her by mail by the students at Spring Hill College, a small Jesuit school in Mobile, Alabama. The questions concentrate largely on the relationship between faith and fiction, her Catholicism, her views of the South and her writing. A complete set of these questions and her answers, as she apparently typed them on her own typewriter, exists among her papers at Georgia College in Milledgeville; they correspond with the published version in a student journal, *The Motley*. Apparently O'Connor found certain advantages in this arrangement. Thereafter she regularly requested questions in advance, or—when all else failed—she made up her own questions and then provided carefully prepared and typed responses to them for the interviewer. Thus she demonstrated her desire to have her ideas presented in as clear and cohesive a fashion as possible.

A certain consistency of habit, discipline, and thought, along with a desire for privacy, characterized O'Connor's responses to others. Experience had taught her that interviewers either will not or cannot record ideas effectively. By continuing to consent to be interviewed, she demonstrated her graciousness as well as, it seems, her eagerness to speak forthrightly; by seeking to control the circumstances of the interview, she revealed both her skepticism of interviews as a means for carefully considered communication and her distrust of the intentions of the interviewer. Perhaps, too, as her letters seem to indicate, she was fearful of her own ability to respond spontaneously to complex questions. She was firm in her beliefs, but she may have lacked assurance in her ability to explain them in a meaningful way orally. She seemed to have trusted more her ability to write answers down.

Although ill for most of her adult life, O'Connor was by no means sedentary. She complained about the ordeal of traveling, but she frequently accepted invitations to visit colleges and to deliver lectures. One of her more pleasant trips occurred when she ventured up to the College of St. Teresa in Winona, Minnesota, where, as she wrote to John Lynch, she had been asked to talk "on being a Cathlick writer an all" (14 June 1959—*HB*, p. 336). Despite their youth, the students there were more adept than some of O'Connor's other, more experienced interviewers at eliciting relaxed and spontaneous responses from her.

O'Connor occasionally complained also about the number of requests for her time or presence, but she clearly derived a certain satisfaction from these interactions and remained—as in almost all things—good-humored about them, even as the effects of the debilitating disease lupus ravaged her body. She seemed particularly to dislike televised or videotaped appearances. In a letter responding to a request to be interviewed for an Atlanta television program, O'Connor declined—stating that some writers should be heard but not seen.[3] On one occasion she complained to "A" about the large number of letters from students asking for her help as they struggled to write their papers and then added sarcastically that she should have earned an honorary doctorate for all of her aid to graduate students (18 April 1959—*HB*, p. 328).

She may have felt similarly about requests from magazines or journals to respond to their inquiries, but she nevertheless often obliged. In 1959 when the editors of *Esprit*, a student publication of the University of Scranton, asked her to submit answers to their questions about the nature of short fiction and thereby to participate in "A Symposium on The Short Story," along with John Updike, J.F. Powers, and Elizabeth Enright, O'Connor agreed. Her answers to the

3. Letter to Dora Byron, 15 July 1962. Special Collections, Woodruff Library, Emory University.

four questions they posed were listed first. A long, mutual relationship developed between O'Connor and *Esprit;* she later published an essay there, and after her death the journal devoted one entire issue to essays and reminiscences about her. Also, in 1961, she contributed to the "Symposium on the Teaching of Creative Writing" in the journal *Four Quarters.* Her response to their survey on creative writing is typically terse—one short paragraph, in sharp contrast to the more lengthy replies of Anthony West, Ray Bradbury, John Knowles, Katherine Anne Porter, and others:

> Unfortunately, there is a kind of writing that can be taught; it is the kind you then have to teach people not to read. This does not mean that writing courses are not valuable, but that their value is limited to doing a few things which will help the student with talent to a greater critical awareness. A good writing course can do two things: show the student what, from the writer's point of view, great literature is and give him time and credit and criticism for writing of his own if his gift seems to merit it. If such a course is directed by an intelligent teacher who is not interested in impressing his own image on the writing of his students, it can be very valuable and can save the student many false starts.[4]

The occasions when O'Connor was a participant in a literary discussion with others may in fact provide the best framework for considering her personality and style. In a symposium at Vanderbilt University and a later panel discussion at Wesleyan College her sharp, succinct answers clearly define her presence. It is worthwhile to contrast her answers with those of Robert Penn Warren, a figure of considerable stature as a poet as well as a writer of fiction and a thoughtful literary critic, who was the other participant at Vanderbilt. O'Connor was much less apt than Warren to refer to other writers or literary works or periods or genres, although it is clear from reading her correspondence and reviews and glancing through her personal library that she was well read. She was more likely to use rural figures of speech, southern idioms, and casual dialogue. In answering a question concerning her technique of writing novels, she replied, "Well, I just kind of feel it out like a hound-dog. I follow the scent." She frequently responded to a question with a brief story of concrete

4. "Symposium on the Teaching of Writing," *Four Quarters* 10 (January 1961), p. 20.

example. Always her perceptions are unique and stated idiosyncratically if not eloquently.

At the Wesleyan panel discussion and in many other instances, O'Connor's well-known dry sense of humor allowed her to poke fun at the questioner, the question, or even herself. When she was preparing to go to Wesleyan, she wrote to John Hawkes that she and Katherine Anne Porter, Caroline Gordon, Madison Jones "are going to be paid (well) to swap cliches about Southern culture" (9 October 1960—*HB*, pp. 412-413). She did not seem to take any of these occasions too seriously; yet she was always well prepared. She had the uncanny ability to see things for what they were and thereby to distance herself from them; yet she could seize the opportunity to make meaningful statements. She was an engaging presence: she was herself actively involved in issues of literature, life, and theology, and she was able to interest others in them as well.

O'Connor was interviewed several times by noted Atlanta writer and journalist Betsy [Lochridge] Fancher. This series, beginning in 1959, is significant for a number of reasons. Among the O'Connor papers in the library at Georgia College at Milledgeville is a complete set of questions and answers on which Lochridge based her first interview. Again, it was extremely important to O'Connor to have her *ideas* presented correctly. She realized how alien and complicated they might seem to the interviewer and subsequent reader, so she often prepared questions and answers in advance. Portions of this initial interview are repeated in subsequent interviews and articles by Fancher. The series further reveals O'Connor's ambivalence toward interviews. Undoubtedly she liked and respected this woman as she maintained a friendship with her and permitted herself to be interviewed on a number of occasions. Nonetheless, she seemed to resent the imposition on her time and privacy, and she distrusted the means and ends of these interviews.

After the first interview with Betsy Lochridge, O'Connor noted in a letter to a friend that she had written down a list of answers to some frequently asked questions for the interviewer in order to guarantee at least a measure of accuracy in the published account. Nonetheless, she was unprepared for one question having to do with the effect of being Catholic on her work: "I said it was a great help. Why? I sputtered out a lot of incoherencies, which I will really hate to see when they appear" (3 October 1959—*HB*, pp. 351-352). She also felt that the photographs accompanying the interview did little to flatter her or her farm. She often worried about how she looked as well as about what she said.

In 1963, she had another encounter with this same interviewer, who consistently paid homage to the writer and her fiction. But O'Connor was upset by the focus of many of the questions on racial issues and by what she felt was a misrepresentation of her ideas when the article appeared in the *Atlanta* magazine. Afterwards she gave a stinging indictment of journalists: "You can't get around newspaper people. I think they are the slobber-heartedest lily-mindedest piously conniving crowd in the modern world" (1 September 1963—*HB*, p. 537). Even though O'Connor was known for her occasionally sharp comments, she was usually more restrained and controlled in her assessment of people. The degree of her anger, directed at someone with whom she had a positive relationship, reflects how important she considered the precise wording of her ideas and the way in which they were presented.

An episode in 1960 with *Time* magazine reinforced O'Connor's anxiety about interviews. After the publication of *The Violent Bear It Away*, some reporters from *Time* visited Milledgeville to talk with her. She felt that they simply wanted her to satisfy their expectations of what it meant to be "southern" and "Catholic." She later worried about her inability to articulate her ideas clearly and feared that she may have sounded as incoherent as Bishop, the retarded child in her novel. The result was a rather cursory review of her novel, not an interview at all. The review upset her, not solely because of the assessment of her novel, but also because it mentioned the fact that she was suffering from lupus which it then misrepresented as "a tuberculous disease of the skin and mucous membranes that forces her to spend part of her life on crutches."[5] She commented in a letter to Maryat Lee that she did not expect the reviewer from *Time* to like the novel "but I do regret their making it and me so unhealthy-sounding" (25 February 1960—*HB*, p. 376). A part of O'Connor was clearly worried about the public perception of her physical as well as literary presence. Her self-consciousness as an artist sometimes

---

5. "God-Intoxicated Hillbillies," *Time* (29 February 1960), p. 118.

extended to a self-consciousness about how she appeared and how she was perceived.

Despite her increasing distrust of interviewers and interviewing situations, O'Connor continued to consent to being interviewed but usually under more carefully controlled conditions. When Margaret Turner, a reporter for the Atlanta newspapers, and some other members of a journalism society bestowing an award on O'Connor traveled to Milledgeville to talk with her, she again apparently either requested questions in advance or composed her own. Among her papers at Georgia College there exists, typed on her own typewriter, a complete set of these questions and answers. The published version remains faithful to this set for the most part. However, some descriptive material is added, and two sets of questions and answers are omitted: one about the importance of southern literature and one about the relationship between religion and fiction.

Yet O'Connor continued to form meaningful and mutual relationships with her interviewers. In 1960, Richard Gilman—who was just making his way as a journalist but who later gained wide recognition as a drama critic—made a visit to Milledgeville that was significant for him and O'Connor. Afterwards O'Connor wrote to "A" about how much she had enjoyed their time together (3 September 1960—*HB*, p. 405). Gilman later published his account of this visit under the name of Robert Donner in the Catholic journal *The Sign*. Then several years after O'Connor's death, in a review of *Mystery and Manners*, Gilman reflected again on their meeting. Both accounts are included in this collection because together they provide real insight into this visit, O'Connor's views, and her influence on an interviewer.

Similarly, O'Connor seemed to have enjoyed thoroughly her relationship with Granville Hicks, who demonstrated in essays and reviews a clear appreciation of her work. She was happy about the outcome of her interview with him in 1962 and about the fact that it was so well received in Milledgeville. The response of her friends and neighbors meant a great deal to her. When the local newspaper reprinted the entire article from *Saturday Review*, she wrote to Hicks that the people in Milledgeville were delighted to have their town favorably compared to Charleston. She saw herself largely in the context of her community: "I'm pleased to be a member of my particular family and to live in Baldwin County in the sovereign State of Georgia, and to see what I can see from here," she proclaimed in a later interview with Gerard Sherry. Although she is frequently accused of portraying her fellow southerners negatively, she was genuinely proud of her heritage.

In addition to O'Connor's enhanced reputation in literary circles, she was quickly gaining in stature among intellectuals and artists in the Catholic community. She was highly regarded as a committed believer and a sound apologist; yet she was well aware of the inadequacies of the Church, and she was a harsh critic of the superficial faith of many Catholics. An avid reader of religious periodicals, she contributed essays to them, reviewed them, and allowed herself to be interviewed for them as well. Three interviews in two of these journals, *The Critic* and *Jubilee,* given near the end of her life provide perhaps the clearest articulation of her beliefs concerning the relationship between her faith and her fiction, but she was by no means pleased by them.

Early in 1961 O'Connor's short story "The Partridge Festival" appeared in the Catholic journal *The Critic.* Later that same year O'Connor reviewed this journal in *The Bulletin,* the newspaper for her diocese to which she contributed regularly:

> The articles on music and the arts are usually better than the articles on literature, which too frequently are about minor Catholic liturgy [literary] figures, or when about non-Catholic writers tend to show that these are Catholic in spite of themselves and therefore acceptable. Fiction is considered by most Catholic readers to be a waste of time, and *The Critic,* which recently began publishing a story or two an issue, has taken a step which may prove dangerous to its circulation.[6]

Then in 1962, Joel Wells, editor of *The Critic,* interviewed O'Connor during a car trip as they traveled by automobile from Chicago to South Bend. In Wells's account of their time together, he seems intrigued with O'Connor's straightforward replies to his queries.

A similar relationship developed between O'Connor and the Catholic journal *Jubilee.* In 1961 she published her introduction to *A*

---

6. *The Presence of Grace and Other Book Reviews by Flannery O'Connor,* compiled by Leo Zuber, edited with an introduction by Carter W. Martin (Athens: The University of Georgia Press, 1983), p. 115. Reprinted from *The Bulletin,* 10 June 1961. Subsequent references to this volume will be cited as *(Presence,* p. _____).

*Memoir of Mary Ann* there. The next year she also reviewed *Jubilee*
for *The Bulletin* where she described it as "a partly pictorial monthly
magazine which should be of interest to those who would like to see
more taste and imagination in popular Catholic journalism than is
usually found there" *(Presence,* p. 137). Then in 1963 Ross Mullins
interviewed and photographed her for *Jubilee.* This entire interview,
with both questions and answers typed on her own typewriter, can
be found among her papers in Milledgeville. It later provided part of
the script for the ABC-TV show "Directions 65: A Tribute to Flannery
O'Connor" which was written by one of her other interviewers,
Richard Gilman.[7]

    O'Connor felt that it was important, then, to support Catholic
publications which were making an effort to bridge the gap between
literary and theological concerns. She remained sensitive, however,
about how she appeared and what she seemed to be saying in
interviews. Her discomfort with her public image became acutely
apparent after the *Jubilee* interview and after another one about the
same time with Gerard Sherry published in *The Critic.* Mr. Sherry
had recently taken over as managing editor of *The Bulletin* (renamed
*The Georgia Bulletin).* O'Connor was unsure of the effects of this
change; she seemed skeptical of his judgment, as a non-southerner,
and of the ability of an outsider to understand the South. Soon after
he began his new job she expressed to "A" her fears that Sherry
would not understand the particularities of the South and that as a
result he would simplistically define the region in meaningless,
abstract, liberal terms (19 January 1963—*HB,* p. 506). Her meeting
with Sherry the next month, however, led her to reconsider her
evaluation; she found him to be a good listener who was "modest
and able" (16 February 1963—*HB,* pp. 508-509). Sherry must have
been similarly impressed with O'Connor because he later asked her
to contribute to the monthly supplement on the arts in the
newspaper, and he then published an interview with her in *The
Critic.*

    After the Mullins and Sherry interviews appeared in print,
O'Connor expressed serious misgivings about interviews to a new-

    7. David Farmer, *Flannery O'Connor: A Descriptive Bibliography* (New York and London:
Garland Publishing, Inc., 1981), p. 117.

found correspondent, Janet McKane: "I hate to deliver opinions. On most things I don't deserve an opinion and on a lot of things I simply don't have an opinion" (19 June 1963—*HB,* pp. 524-525). She felt troubled by the way her words sounded in print and believed that the photographs accompanying the *Jubilee* article made her look like she was overburdened by cares and made her home appear desolate. While the pictures in *The Critic* may have been a little better, she thought the interview represented her ideas poorly. The interviews must have continued to disturb her greatly, for later that same month she asked McKane to evaluate her answers. She herself declared them to be "all half-answers, elliptical, incomplete" (30 June 1963—*HB,* p. 527). She added that she was not sure why one of the photographs, a picture of a water tower, was included with the interview—but the photographer "probably thought it symbolized something." Here she was expressing irritation at the incessant effort of some of her readers to try to uncover a close symbolic correspondence between her fiction and life.

That O'Connor's audience was wide and varied is further demonstrated by the account of a meeting published in the *Plymouth Traveler,* a travel magazine for the owners of Plymouth automobiles. An enterprising reporter who had written for some Catholic presses journeyed to Milledgeville to talk with O'Connor about a subject at least as interesting to her as writing or literature: peacocks. Not at all surprisingly, her observations of their habits were precise, detailed and humorous. Above all, she seems fascinated by their stubbornness and perversity.

The types of journals in which O'Connor's interviews appear, then, range from trade magazines to small Catholic publications to regional newspapers to widely regarded magazines. Her interviewers included people with national reputations (Harvey Breit, Granville Hicks, Richard Gilman) and some with a more limited audience. Many of her interviews are fugitive—that is, they appear in little-known magazines or in journals that are now out of print. Given in a time just prior to the technical sophistication currently available to interviewers, a significant number are published in a narrative, descriptive fashion rather than according to a straightforward question-and-answer format. These are, strictly speaking, records of conversations rather than formal interviews. In this collection they are all reprinted exactly as they were first published in order to preserve their original context and texture. For the most part, they are arranged chronologically according to the dates they took place or, if that information was not available, according to the date of publication.

Although expressed in a particular time and place, Flannery O'Connor's fiction embodied and revealed universal ideas. Her curiosity about human nature and its various manifestations compelled her to explore new places. Despite her short life and prolonged illness, she was interviewed in a variety of times and locations. Yet circumstances did not seem to matter much to O'Connor; her approach and behavior remained consistent. Her confidence in herself, in her enterprise as a writer, and in her beliefs—her self-knowledge was always apparent. She could penetrate the surfaces; she could see things in depth. A somewhat shy person whose fiction had a decidedly regional emphasis and location, she was able to hold her own in settings ranging from New York City to Minnesota to Tennessee to Atlanta to her home turf of Milledgeville. She may have been "stuck with the South" as she proudly proclaimed to Betsy [Lochridge] Fancher in one interview, but her perceptions were wide-ranging and insightful. Further, she was able to communicate her beliefs and ideas to university students and professors, journalists, Catholic clerics and laypeople alike. Thus her interviews, given sparingly but with careful reflection and precision, make a unique contribution to an understanding of the stories told by O'Connor and to the evolving narrative of her short but influential life.

I wish to express my appreciation to Alan Clark and the other members of the Reference Department of Woodruff Library, Emory University, for their assistance in finding and collecting these interviews. Also, Nancy Davis of the Ina Dillard Russell Library at Georgia College was consistently helpful and cordial. For their willingness to talk with me at length about O'Connor and her work, I wish to thank Sally Fitzgerald and Sarah Gordon. For his support of this and other projects, I am grateful to David L. Minter; for his generosity and assistance I am grateful to L. Ray Patterson of the Emory University School of Law. I am, of course, indebted to the interviewers and writers represented in this collection and to their publishers for granting me permission to reprint the interviews. Finally, I wish to thank my editor, Seetha Srinivasan for her persistence; my colleague, Nancy-Laurel Pettersen, for her kindness; my husband, Ron Grapevine, for his presence; my daughter, Rebecca Rose Magee Grapevine, for her inspiration; and my teacher, Floyd C. Watkins, for his friendship.

RMM
June 1986

# Chronology

1925       March 25: Mary Flannery O'Connor born to Edward
           Francis and Regina Cline O'Connor in Savannah,
           Georgia.

1938       O'Connor family moved from Savannah to Milledgeville,
           Georgia.

1941       Edward O'Connor died of lupus erythematosus.

1942       Flannery O'Connor graduated from Peabody High
           School.

1945       Flannery O'Connor graduated from the Georgia State
           College for Women in Milledgeville (later Georgia
           College) with a B.A. in social science.

1945-47    Attended Writer's Workshop, University of Iowa. Received
           Master of Fine Arts.

1946       First short story published: "The Geranium" in *Accent*.

1948-49    Resided at Yaddo in Saratoga Springs, New York.

1950       December: Became seriously ill with what was later
           diagnosed as lupus.

1951       Flannery and Regina O'Connor moved to Andalusia, a
           dairy farm near Milledgeville. Flannery convalesced and
           began raising peafowl.

1952      Publication of *Wise Blood*

1953      Received the *Kenyon Review* Fellowship in Fiction.

1954      Reappointed Kenyon Fellow.

1955      Publication of *A Good Man is Hard to Find*

1957      Grant from the National Institute of Arts and Letters; O.
          Henry Award—1st Prize Story: "Greenleaf"

1959      $10,000 grant from the Ford Foundation

1960      Publication of *The Violent Bear it Away*

1962      *Wise Blood* reissued with "Author's Note."
          Publication of *A Memoir of Mary Ann,* for which
          O'Connor wrote the introduction, by the Dominican
          Nuns of Our Lady of Perpetual Help Cancer Home in
          Atlanta.
          Litt.D. from St. Mary's College

1963      O. Henry Award—1st Prize Story: "Everything That Rises
          Must Converge."
          Litt.D. from Smith College

1964      3 August: Flannery O'Connor died in Milledgeville.

1965      Publication of *Everything That Rises Must Converge*;
          O. Henry Award—1st Prize Story: "Revelation."

1969      Publication of *Mystery and Manners: The Occasional
          Prose of Flannery O'Connor*

1971      Publication of *The Complete Stories of Flannery
          O'Connor*; winner of a posthumous National Book Award

1979        Publication of *The Habit of Being: Letters of Flannery O'Connor*

1983        Publication of *The Presence of Grace and Other Book Reviews by Flannery O'Connor*

1985        Publication of *Flannery O'Connor's Library: Resources of Being*

# Conversations with Flannery O'Connor

# May 15 Is Publication Date of Novel by Flannery O'Connor, Milledgeville

*The Union-Recorder*/April 1952

From *The Union-Recorder* [Milledgeville, GA], 24 April 1952, 1.

Harcourt, Brace and Company, one of the country's leading publishing houses, has announced May 15 as the publication date for *Wise Blood*, a novel by Flannery O'Connor of Milledgeville.

Although advance copies of the book are not yet available, a prepublication review of it by the New York critic, Caroline Gordon, says in part: "I was more impressed by *Wise Blood* than any novel I have read in a long time. Her picture of the modern world is literally terrifying. Kafka is almost the only one of our contemporaries who has achieved such effects."

Editorial comment by the publishers describes the book as an "extraordinary novel, which introduces an important new talent, relating the story of Hazel Motes, who comes from Eastrod, Tennessee, and has discovered a new religion which he preaches from the hood of his rat-colored Essex. . . . Haze, a primitive figure, represents the most primitive issue of our time or any time—religion. In his fight for truth as he sees it, he clashes with two other evangelists. . . ."

*Wise Blood* say the publishers, "has great humor, and horror, and compassion, and its satire is reminiscent of the Evelyn Waugh of *The Loved One.*

Although a native of Savannah, the 26-year-old author of the new book is a member of the Cline family of Milledgeville and in 1938 returned here with her mother, Mrs. Edward O'Connor, and she completed high school at Peabody and her college studies at Georgia State College for Women. From GSCW she went to the State

University of Iowa and studied writing under Paul Engle, receiving a
Master of Fine Arts in Literature in 1947. She had a fellowship in
English at Iowa for two years.

She began her novel in 1947, living for seven months of that year
at Yaddo, Saratoga Springs, N.Y., which is an estate left by the Trask
family for writers, painters and musicians who are doing creative
work. Later she lived in the country with friends in Connecticut.

Back in Milledgeville for the past year, Miss O'Connor is living for
the present with her mother at "Andalusia," a rambling, storybook
farm owned by the Cline family.

"I write every day for at least two hours," says the young author,
"and I spend the rest of my time largely in the society of ducks."
Raising ducks is her hobby and she owns, also, geese, pheasants,
quails and one frizzly chicken. A frizzly chicken, she explained, is a
chicken that looks more like a wet fur coat than anything else.

Miss O'Connor's interest in feathered friends dates back to the time
she was about 11 years old and she owned a chicken that got in
*Pathé News* by the simple (but exceedingly singular) procedure of
walking backwards. A *Pathe* cameraman traveled across several states
to film the hen that went places in reserve with as much ease as most
birds stroll forward. "Since that big event," remarked the chicken's
proud owner as she looked back on the excitement of that by-gone
day, "my life has been an anti-climax."

She gives credit to an advertisement in the *Union-Recorder* for an
idea that led to one of the chapters in her book. A local theater
offered free passes to fans who would shake hands with a gorilla
appearing here "in person" on the day of the particular film's
showing. This chapter happens to be one of the several printed as
separate stories in various literary magazines prior to publication of
her novel.

Flannery O'Connor's first story was published in *Accent* in 1946.
Since then she has had stories or chapters of her novel in such
publications as *Sewanee Review, Partisan Review, Mademoiselle,
Tomorrow,* and *New World Writing*. She writes only fiction and is
interested in the novel only as art.

Her book is dedicated to her mother.

# Galley Proof:
## *A Good Man Is Hard to Find*
Harvey Breit/1955

Transcript of the *Galley Proof* program filmed by WRCA-TV (NBC) in New York in May 1955. Permission to transcribe and print excerpt from *Galley Proof* courtesy of The National Broadcasting Co., Inc. © 1985 The National Broadcasting Company, Inc. All rights reserved.

A WRCA-TV Workshop presents "Galley Proof," a program about books, today featuring a dramatization from the galley proof of Flannery O'Connor's forthcoming collection of short stories, *A Good Man is Hard to Find*. Now meet your host, Harvey Breit, Assistant Editor of the Book Section of the *New York Times*, by-liner of the popular weekly column "In & Out of Books" and author of "There Falls Tom Fool."

**Breit:** Good afternoon. This is a galley proof. This is a book before it is a book. This program, "Galley Proof," to me brings together one of the oldest means of communication—books—and one of the youngest—television. Books, good books, that stimulate the mind and affect the heart, are strong. They endure. Each time a new medium comes into our lives—movies, radio, television—people say, "the reading of books is finished." It is not true. Books do get read. It is entirely possible that they are getting read more than ever and that television is a friend, and not an enemy. At least a number of librarians have pointed out that dramatizations of novels create a rush for those novels in their libraries. We accept this fact of an amiable union between literature and television, and "Galley Proof" is an attempt to bring forward in advance, as a kind of preview, the most exciting new books we know of. Such a book is a collection of short stories, *A Good Man is Hard to Find*, to be published this Friday. The author is Flannery O'Connor. Several years ago she wrote a novel,

*Wise Blood*, which critics hailed as a brilliant book. One critic called her "perhaps the most naturally gifted of the youngest generation of American novelists." Here she is, Flannery O'Connor.

**Breit:** Miss O'Connor, could you tell us a little bit about yourself?

**O'Connor:** Well, Mr. Breit, I'm a Georgian, and I was educated in Georgia and in Iowa, and I've been writing for about ten years.

**Breit:** Yes. Well, what schools did you go to?

**O'Connor:** Well, I went to the Georgia State College for Women and the University of Iowa.

**Breit:** What is at the University of Iowa? Is that the creative writing courses there?

**O'Connor:** There is a workshop there for writers.

**Breit:** Is that the school that Paul Engle runs?

**O'Connor:** Yes.

**Breit:** Did you write before you went to the University of Iowa?

**O'Connor:** Oh, just a little, for my own amusement, but not professionally.

**Breit:** Then at the University of Iowa, did you begin to write short stories?

**O'Connor:** Then I began to write short stories, publicly.

**Breit:** How did the novel come about?

**O'Connor:** Well, I thought I had better get to working on a novel, so I got to work and wrote one.

**Breit:** Could you tell us a little about that novel? I mean, was it a difficult stretch for you, and how long did you take to work on it?

**O'Connor:** Well, I worked on it for five years.

**Breit:** Where did you work on it? Did you work on it in Georgia? Or in Iowa?

**O'Connor:** Oh, in Georgia, then New York, and then Iowa. . . .

**Breit:** Yes. I understand you are living on a farm.

**O'Connor:** Yes. I only live on one, though. I don't see much of it. I'm a writer, and I'm far from the rocking chair.

**Breit:** Do you have a fixed pattern of work?

**O'Connor:** Yes, I work every morning.

**Breit:** . . . and you don't miss a day?

**O'Connor:** No, not even Sunday.

**Breit:** Is there a discipline involved or does it come naturally to you?

**O'Connor:** Well, the discipline doesn't come naturally to me, but I've had to develop it.

**Breit:** Yes. Well, I remember that Thomas Mann once said that he hated writing, but it was a trap that he had fallen into. Do you feel that at all?

**O'Connor:** Well, I think you hate it, and you love it, too. It's something—when you can't do anything else you have to do that.

**Breit:** It is a kind of inevitable thing.

**O'Connor:** Yes.

**Breit:** Well, I think, Flannery, that out of your book, *A Good Man is Hard to Find*, we have selected a story, "The Life You Save May Be Your Own." And, out of these galley proofs, we do have that story. I'd like to read some of it to you, if you can stand it, and the audience.

(Dramatization)

**Breit:** We'll go back to it in a few minutes. Myself, I wish we didn't have to leave it. Miss O'Connor, what do you think? Did you enjoy seeing it?

**O'Connor:** Yes, I wish we didn't have to leave it too.

**Breit:** Well we agree! What about some of those fascinating characters? Do you know them at all? Have you seen people like that?

**O'Connor:** Well, no, not really. I've seen many people like that, I think, and I've seen myself. I think, putting all that together you get these people.

**Breit:** Yes. I wondered this: these days we hear about Southern writers a great deal, sort of a renaissance of southern writers. There is Mr. William Faulkner, who has won a Nobel prize; Erskine Caldwell has been a great figure for a while; Katherine Anne Porter came from the South; and Eudora Welty, Carson McCullers, Tennessee Williams, and Truman Capote. Is there something to being a Southerner in terms of literature?

**O'Connor:** I think it's easier for a Southerner to begin writing than for anyone from almost any other section of the country, because we have so many conventions and so much tension in the South. We have a content to begin on.

**Breit:** Somebody once tried to relate the South as it exists now and in the past twenty years to the Russia of the late 19th century, where a great novel came out with Tolstoy and Dostoevsky, and Gogol, and Turgenev, and Chekhov. That there was the same type of situation—a great tension and a great impact of the new social life on the old conventions. Do you think there's something in that?

**O'Connor:** I think there is.

**Breit:** Do you think, too, that a Northerner, for example, reading this and seeing this, would have as much appreciation of the people in your book, your stories, as a Southerner?

**O'Connor:** Yes, I think perhaps more, because he at least wouldn't be distracted by the Southern thinking that this was a novel about the South, or a story about the South, which it is not.

**Breit:** You don't feel that it is?

**O'Connor:** No.

**Breit:** I don't either. Why don't you?

**O'Connor:** Well, simply because a serious novelist is in pursuit of reality. And of course when you're a Southerner and in pursuit of reality, the reality you come up with is going to have a Southern accent, but that's just an accent; it's not the essence of what you're trying to do.

**Breit:** There is the fact that in knowing something minutely, you seem to know everything. I mean, one does use one's own knowledge, one's knowledge of one's environment, but it doesn't stay with that environment.

**O'Connor:** I think that to overcome regionalism, you must have a great deal of self-knowledge. I think to know yourself is to know your region, and that it's also to know the world, and in a sense, paradoxically, it's also to be in exile from that world. So that you have a great deal of detachment.

**Breit:** We're going to exile you right now and take you back to "Galley Proof" and to the show. Shall we? Can we call it a show? (Dramatization)

**Breit:** It isn't over. What we're seeing now is only part of the story, "The Life You Save May Be Your Own." Flannery, would you like to tell our audience what happens in that story?

**O'Connor:** No, I certainly would not. I don't think you can paraphrase a story like that. I think there's only one way to tell it and that's the way it is told in the story.

**Breit:** That's a sound, for me, pure statement. It's like asking

Cézanne or Matisse to repaint their picture in order to explain it to you. Or something of that kind. Do you think, however, since we can't say or talk about the outcome of it, what does a writer try to do in a short story? Or what does a writer try to do in a novel? What is the secret of writing?

**O'Connor:** Well, I think that a serious fiction writer describes an action only in order to reveal a mystery. Of course, he may be revealing the mystery to himself at the same time as he is revealing it to everyone else. He may not even succeed in revealing it to himself, but I think he must sense its presence at least.

**Breit:** So that in writing the story, are you experiencing a mystery? I mean, is it a mystery to you?

**O'Connor:** It's generally a mystery to me, I think.

**Breit:** Yes. In a sense, even, isn't it possible that a story will do things that you don't expect it to do?

**O'Connor:** Yes. Yes, all the time.

**Breit:** And so that in one way, writing a story is a kind of self-knowledge, really.

**O'Connor:** Yes.

**Breit:** With greater discovery of oneself, [one can] know the whole world. I wonder, for example, in talking about how a story comes out, why it is that audiences go and see *Hamlet* over and over again. There isn't so much to this whole idea of suspense, is there?

**O'Connor:** No.

**Breit:** I mean, it's possible, for example, to see something over and over again, to know the outcome of the story, and yet it will hold you over and over again so that something about what you say about a mystery is true.

**O'Connor:** The style is about the only thing that can really be fresh in the story. That's the reason the story can get that.

**Breit:** I'm struck, in your stories, for myself, and I say this with absolute honesty, that your stories are extremely honest. I mean, if one could qualify honesty. I don't feel that a line is out of place; everything in it is right and homogenous. There isn't one alien line. How do you get that? Is it a marriage of your own sense of yourself and your craft?

**O'Connor:** Well, it's something that I certainly couldn't explain as a writer. I . . . .

**Breit:** There is a distance, in my mind, and I think T.S. Eliot, in one of his poems, says it, that there is a great distance between the idea and the act. Between what the author conceives in his mind and what is the act itself, the act of writing, what comes out on a page. There is a great gap, and if I can honor you, I say that that is your great gift. It seems to me that you have annihilated that distance between what's in the mind and what is on the page. Do you—are you pleased by that?

**O'Connor:** I'm pleased, but I don't know how to explain it.

**Breit:** I know, but I mean, does that sound relevant to you—to what you're doing?

**O'Connor:** Yes.

**Breit:** And I, for myself, think that although Miss O'Connor can be called a Southern writer, I agree that she is not a Southern writer, just as Faulkner isn't and that they are, for want of a better term, universal writers, writing about all mankind and about relationships and the mystery of relationships. I think that for me the distinction of Miss O'Connor is not the oblique, refined style that we're getting so much these days. I'm relieved that you write as simply as you do. I think it may have come out in this small dramatization. Do you think so?

**O'Connor:** Yes, I think . . . .

**Breit:** I hope so. I'd like to say thank you. And can we go over and see our actors?

# In and Out of Books: Visitor
Harvey Breit/June 1955

From *The New York Times*, 12 June 1955, p. 8. © 1955 by The
New York Times Company. Reprinted by permission.
After his interview with Flannery O'Connor, Harvey Breit sum-
marized their conversation in a portion of his column "In and Out
of Books."

The youthful author Flannery O'Connor doesn't get to New York
very often. She lives on a farm outside Milledgeville, Ga., and it's a
far piece. The geographical distance isn't as far, though, as the
mental one. Miss O'Connor is a writer and writes every day, even on
Sundays. Making trips is an interruption. She is 30, was born in
Savannah, graduated from Georgia State College for Women, then
went on to the U. of Iowa, where she took the school's writing course
for two years.

Up until that time Miss O'Connor says she wrote but not for
publication. During Iowa she began to sell her short stories. Still and
nevertheless, and maybe in spite of, her first book was a novel, highly
praised, titled *Wise Blood*. Now Miss O'Connor has published a
collection of stories, *A Good Man Is Hard to Find*, and in case you
have jumped from the first page to this one, go back, reader, to page
5, where you will find an appraisal of the book.

We asked Miss O'Connor if she worked on her farm and she said
quietly (but with quiet fervor), "No, I'm a writer." She told us she
raised peacocks (some of them walk around in some of her stories),
but we balked at asking her if she had a personal hand in it. She
believes that what the writer needs the most is self-knowledge, that in
knowing yourself you know everything, or nearly everything, about
people. She doesn't think of herself as a Southern writer. "My people
could come from anywhere," she told us, "but naturally since I know
the South, they speak with a Southern accent." Which they do. They
also speak with the simplicity of truth, and with its color and nuance.

11

# Baboons Differ with Giraffes
Celestine Sibley/February 1957

That prize-winning short story writer, Miss Flannery O'Connor, came up from her home in Milledgeville the other night to speak of writers and writing at Emory University.

It was her first appearance here since her short story, "Green Leaf," won the O. Henry Award—and despite her scorching scorn for amateurs and people who write mostly to "fill their pockets," she was the hit of the season. (This is new proof to me of the amazing tolerance and resilience of people who are interested in writing. They join clubs and sign up for courses, paying some money at both places to bring in speakers who tell them how ridiculous writers' clubs and courses are!)

Not that the quiet, shy-seeming Miss O'Connor was so blunt as all that. She did compare the Emory course to a sort of portable zoo, wherein the animals appear one at a time "and what the giraffe says this week will be contradicted by the baboon next week." And she did say she had no use for amateur writers' clubs "where amateurs criticize amateurs with 50 per cent flattery and 50 per cent ignorance."

But her fierce and single-minded devotion to good writing, her intelligence and unrelenting honesty, gave everything she said value and made it not only palatable but altogether captivating to those of us who are either earnest amateurs or seekers after a fast buck.

The fact that Miss O'Connor's works appear almost exclusively in the literary reviews of small circulation, rather than in the big, bright, slick, one-on-every-coffee-table national magazines, shows that she practices what she preaches—good but poorly paid writing. And when she talks of it she doesn't prattle about working habits, whether to use a typewriter or a ball-point pen, "techniques" or how to find an agent. She talks purely and simply about writing.

Beginning writers, said Miss O'Connor, are "concerned with unfleshed ideas and emotions." And then she set about showing how to put flesh on both with concrete, rather than abstract, writing. She doesn't think writing can be learned in the absence of talent, but she does think that teachers who criticize manuscripts and lead you to the right kind of reading are helpful.

"If you want to write well and live well at the same time you better arrange to inherit money," she said acidly.

"Few people who are interested in writing are interested in writing well," she said. "They are interested in getting something published or making a killing. They are interested in BEING a writer."

She quoted a man who said writing a novel was like "giving birth to a sideways piano," made laughing references to people who fear symbolism as "a sort of literary Masonic grip," and spoke of the "certain fine-grained stupidity" required of a storyteller. She believes that "more happens in modern fiction with less furor" than used to happen in stories and spoke of readers who enjoy fiction because "their sense of mystery is deepened by contact with reality and their sense of reality is deepened by contact with mystery."

Writing fiction, she said, is "poorly paid and liberally misunderstood," and when that and the other obstacles are made clear any student who perseveres is "either talented or nuts," she said.

Of her own writing she said little, except that she works at it about two hours a day and has no other job, that she lets her characters carry her along, not knowing "until I get there—or nearly there" what the end will be.

# *Motley* Special: Interview with Flannery O'Connor
## *The Motley/1958*

From *The Motley* [Spring Hill College, Mobile, AL] 9 (Spring 1958), 29-31. Reprinted by permission.

Correspondence to questions by students. The questions asked represent a recent student discussion held at the invitation of *The Motley* staff. The answers are a proxy report of Miss O'Connor's opinions.

**Q.** Should Catholic fiction writers write for a Catholic audience?

**A.** No. Not enough Catholics read good fiction. To write for a Catholic audience would mean that the writer would either 1) have to write down, or 2) starve to death. Neither is advisable.

**Q.** How does the writer or reader recognize the Catholic audience in this country?

**A.** There's no accurate way to track it down, but you can form your own opinion from reading the type of fiction printed and recommended in the more popular Catholic magazines and by talking with Catholics about books. The Catholic audience in this country is probably improving in taste but it has a far piece to go.

**Q.** How much influence do the "pious" reviewers, lay and religious, exert?

**A.** None, except on a few old ladies.

**Q.** Can the Church be accused of intolerance in censorship? Can Catholics defend their church's policy agreeably? Do they?

**A.** Principle should be distinguished from policy. The Church has a right to legislate these matters for Catholics by way of the Bishops, the Index and the Canon law that concerns reading. In this she legislates for the majority and if this works a hardship on the better qualified, they have to put up with it. Permissions can usually be had to read what is needed. Whether one can defend this agreeably

14

depends on how agreeable one is. People who do not believe that
the Church is a Divine institution can seldom be convinced that any
restrictions are justified. Perhaps a few Catholics try to defend the
Church in this but it is uphill work. Legislation from the official
Church is one thing; ladies' committees to purify the drugstore
bookracks are another. They are usually manned by incompetents,
create ill will, and scare interested people away from the Church.

**Q.** What do you consider the more desirable forms of nature
expressed in fiction?

**A.** All fiction is about human nature. What kind of human nature
you write about depends on the amount and kind of your talent, not
on what you may consider correct behaviour to be. The best forms of
behaviour are not more desirable than the worst for fiction if the
writer sees the situation he is creating under the aspect of Truth and
follows the necessities of his art.

**Q.** Is the Southern Catholic more insular and more excessively
pious than Catholics elsewhere? If you think so, is that one reason
why art is so poorly patronized in the Catholic South?

**A.** I doubt if Catholics in the South are more insular or more pious
than Catholics in other sections. Insularity seems to be a general
Catholic failing in this country. If art is poorly patronized in the South,
a great deal of art is nevertheless coming out of the South and there
are some Catholics among those producing it. The lack of patronage
of the arts is probably because of poor education.

**Q.** Can a novelist shade his prejudices without seeming deceitful?

**A.** Every writer has a point of view. In fiction, judging and seeing
should be one act as nearly as possible. Unfairness in seeing is easily
detectable and cannot be got away with.

**Q.** When did you discover that writing was your vocation? How?

**A.** A certain amount of publication is usually sufficient to convince
a writer that writing is his vocation. This combined with an inability to
do anything else is a foolproof indication. I never thought about the
matter one way or the other.

**Q.** How much entertainment should a critical reader get from a
novel? How much of the entertaining should be in the novelist's plan?

**A.** This depends on what you mean by entertainment. If you
mean pleasure for the mind, the answer is 100% in both cases. If you
mean amusement, none is necessary.

**Q.** Is humor as scarce as seriousness in Catholic writing?

**A.** Mighty scarce it is; but there is J. F. Powers with both.

**Q.** Can a short story afford to be definitive on modern life?

**A.** A short story can do so much and no more. It takes a limited situation and tries to explore it to bring out what meaning there is in it. I doubt if it can be definitive of anything but what it sets up, i.e., a particular happening.

**Q.** How should points of view like those of Wylie be studied by Catholics?

**A.** Mr. Wylie is not so deep that he requires study; however, a lot of people think the way he does and it is just as well to know how the other half thinks.

**Q.** Where is the Catholic writer's best subject matter to be found?

**A.** This depends on what he knows and where he comes from. Subject matter has more to do with region than religion, at least in fiction.

**Q.** How far does a sense of mystery enter into a novel of the Greene type?

**A.** The sense of mystery is apparent in all good fiction and Mr. Greene seems to produce it better than most.

**Q.** Under what aspects is obscenity treated most effectively?

**A.** Obscenity is obscenity. If you can consider it as treated under "aspects" I suppose you would say that it is best treated under the aspect of art, that is, used where it contributes to the delineation of character or situation, but never where it draws attention to itself and away from the plan of the work.

# A Symposium on the Short Story
*Esprit*/Winter 1959

From *Esprit* [University of Scranton, Scranton, PA], 3 (Winter 1959), 8-13. © 1959 by University of Scranton.

Flannery O'Connor, John Updike, Elizabeth Enright, and J.F. Powers were each asked two questions:
1. What is a Short Story? 2. What advice do you give to the college student interested in writing—especially the Short Story?
O'Connor's answers are reprinted here.

1. This is a hellish question inspired by the devil who tempts textbook publishers. I have been writing stories for fifteen years without a definition of one. The best I can do is tell you what a story is not.

   1) It is not a joke.

   2) It is not an anecdote.

   3) It is not a lyric rhapsody in prose.

   4) It is not a case history.

   5) It is not a reported incident.

It is none of these things because it has an extra dimension and I think this extra dimension comes about when the writer puts us in the middle of some human action and shows it as it is illuminated and outlined by mystery. In every story there is some minor revelation which, no matter how funny the story may be, gives us a hint of the unknown, of death.

2. My advice is to start reading and writing and looking and listening. Pay less attention to yourself than to what is outside you and if you must write about yourself, get a good distance away and judge yourself with a stranger's eyes and a stranger's severity.

Remember that reason should always go where the imagination goes. The artist uses his reason to discover an answering reason in everything he sees. For him, to be reasonable is to find in the object, in the situation, in the sequence, the spirit which makes it itself.

The short story writer particularly has to learn to read life in a way that includes the most possibilities—like the medieval commentators on scripture, who found three kinds of meaning in the literal level of the sacred text. If you see things in depth, you will be more liable to write them that way.

# An Interview with Flannery O'Connor and Robert Penn Warren
Vagabond/23 April 1959

From Vagabond [Vanderbilt University] 4 (February 1960),
9-17. Reprinted by permission of Vanderbilt University.

On the morning of April 23, 1959, Miss O'Connor and
Mr. Warren met with several students and faculty members for a recorded interview. Among the participants
were Joe Sills, Jr., Cyrus Hoy, Edwin Godsey, Randall
Mize, Walter Sullivan, Harry Minetree, Jim Whitehead,
Bill Harrison, Tom McNair, Betty Weber, Walter Russell,
George Core and Chris Boner. The interview was edited by Cyrus Hoy and Walter Sullivan, and is printed
through the courtesy of the Vanderbilt English department.

**Mr. Sills:** I would like to ask either or both of you: when you set out
to write a story, how much of an outline do you have? I am of the
opinion that if you outline something rather fully, it is very possible
for you to be paralyzed creatively, to become a kind of reporter of
what you've outlined. How do you handle it yourself or is it a
problem at all?

**Miss O'Connor:** I just don't outline.

**Mr. Warren:** I had an outline once, and it took me two years to
pull out of it. You think you've got your work done.

**Mr. Sills:** What about the novel? How much outline do you work
from? How do you write a novel?

**Miss O'Connor:** Well, I just kind of feel it out like a hound-dog. I
follow the scent. Quite frequently it's the wrong scent, and you stop
and go back to the last plausible point and start in some other
direction.

**Mr. Sills:** Are you aware of how it is going to end?

**Miss O'Connor:** Not always. You know the direction you're going in, but you don't know how you'll get there.

**Mr. Hoy:** May I ask, Miss O'Connor, did you know how "A Good Man is Hard to Find" was going to end?

**Miss O'Connor:** Yes, I knew. I anticipated.

**Mr. Godsey:** Do any of you begin with the theme first, and hunt for the story, or do you do it the other way around?

**Miss O'Connor:** I think it's better to begin with the story, and then you know you've got something. Because the theme is more or less something that's in you, but if you intellectualize it too much you probably destroy your novel.

**Mr. Warren:** People have done it the other way, in cases: starting out with an idea, and hunting the fable, as they used to say. Coleridge is a good example of it. He says he had his theme for "The Ancient Mariner" for years. He kept casting around for the appropriate fable. He even made a false start or two, until he hit the right story. Those are not contradictory things, I think, because the theme was in him. He had at least reached some pretty clear intellectual definition of it before he started.

**Mr. Godsey:** Theoretically, which do you think is better for the young writer?

**Mr. Warren:** Let's don't say "the young writer." Just drop that phrase; not just for here, for always. Any writer who is not young had better shut up shop. He'd better be trying to wrangle through what he is up to, and pretend he's young anyway, or quit. Once he thinks he's an old writer who knows, he's finished. About which is better: I don't think there's any choice in the matter. It's just a matter of temperament. I think people can freeze themselves by their hasty intellectualizing of what they are up to.

**Mr. Mize:** Miss O'Connor, I heard a really wonderful story about how you came to name "The Artificial Nigger," and I wonder if you would tell us about that?

**Miss O'Connor:** Well, I never had heard the phrase before, but my mother was out trying to buy a cow, and she rode up the country a-piece. She had the address of a man who was supposed to have a cow for sale, but she couldn't find it, so she stopped in a small town and asked the countryman on the side of the road where this house was, and he said, "Well, you go into this town and you can't miss it

'cause it's the only house in town with a artificial nigger in front of it."
So I decided I would have to find a story to fit that. A little lower level
than starting with the theme.

**Mr. Sullivan:** You wrote the story after you had the title? Did you
hit it on the first try? The first time when you tried to fit the title to the
story, did it fit?

**Miss O'Connor:** Well, the title was so dominant.

**Mr. Warren:** Hard to live up to it.

**Miss O'Connor:** Then, when I sent the story to Mr. Ransom, he
said, "Well, we'd better not use this title. You know, it's a tense
situation. We don't want to hurt anybody's feelings." I stood out for
my title.

**Mr. Sullivan:** Red, to get back to this novel business: your books
are awfully well put together. The opening sequences contain so
many images of the book as a whole, and prepare for so many things
to happen. You've got to know a whole lot or you couldn't write that
way.

**Mr. Warren:** There's no law that makes you put the first chapter
first, though.

**Mr. Sullivan:** Well, I know, but . . .

**Mr. Warren:** Some of them have been written first, yes. I don't
think it's knowing how the story comes out that's the point. As
Flannery just said, you know what you want it to feel like. You
envisage the feeling. You may or may not know how it is going to
come out. You may have your big scenes in mind before you start.
You may even be moving toward them all the time. You don't know
whether they will jell out or not jell out. But it seems to me the
important thing is to have enough feeling envisaged and pre-felt, as it
were, about the way the book's going to go. If that feeling isn't there:
unless it dominates your thinking, somehow . . . you know, be the
thing that is behind the muse, the thing that keeps it under control: if
you ever lose that feeling, then you start floundering. But as long as
that feeling as to how the book is going to end is there, something is
guiding it. And then your mechanical problems have a sort of built-in
correction for error. I mean, you have fifty ideas, but somehow you
know they're wrong. If you keep this feeling firmly in you . . . I don't
know how you will it . . . but as long as it is there, you have
something to guide you in this automatic process of trial and error.

You know what the book ought to feel like. Of course you're going to modify that feeling.

**Mr. Sullivan:** I know exactly what you're saying, and I think you're exactly right. But it seems to me that there is a considerable danger in not knowing enough about where you're going, especially in so far as the structure of the book is concerned. In *All the King's Men*, did you write the first chapter first?

**Mr. Warren:** No, it was the second chapter originally. There was a shift in material there which the editor did. The present opening chapter was the second chapter, or part of the second chapter. The original opening got off to a very poor start with the narrator talking about the first time he had seen Stark, the politician. He goes back into the scene which now appears later, in the second or third chapter, when he comes into town to get a political favor, make a political connection, in a restaurant or beer hall in New Orleans. There is this portrait of him coming in, the boy with the Christmas tie, you know, and his hat in his hand. Well, that was a very predictable kind of start. It had no urgency in it. So expository in the worst sense. I was trying to step that up by a kind of commentary on it, and the commentary was pretty crude, and that's the way the thing remained when it went to the publisher. And Lambert Davis said, "Look here, this is a very poor way to start a novel. You've got a natural start in the second chapter, and what's in the first chapter that's important, you can absorb very readily." And I think he was right. I know he was right about its being bad.

**Mr. Sullivan:** Well now look, when you started the book, certainly you knew that Judge Irvin had been very culpable in his financial dealings.

**Mr. Warren:** No, I did not. No, I didn't know it at all. That came quite a while along the way.

**Mr. Sullivan:** Well then, did you know that Allen Stanton was going to kill Willie?

**Mr. Warren:** Yes, I knew that.

**Mr. Sullivan:** You knew that Sugar Boy was going to kill Allen?

**Mr. Warren:** Yes. The point is, I am mixing up two things, the novel and the verse play which preceded it. There you had the germ: the politician, his wife, his mistress, her brother were in the play. It was a very small cast, you see, and then it became a novel, but there was no Judge Irvin in the play at all. There's no mother, nothing of that personal stuff. In fact, there was no Jack Burden. He came in as a nameless newspaperman with two sentences to speak, a boyhood friend without a name as the assassin is waiting for Stark, who is then called Taylor. The newspaperman just meets this man and says "Hello, Hello," just a few words between them, a way of killing time, of having a little nostalgic reference to their boyhood. Kind of a hold, you know, until the action could happen. You've always got to do that, you know. If a man goes to kill a man, if a man goes to get an ice cream soda, you can't just let him go and get it, or go and kill him. You have to stop it, hold it a minute, distract it a little, delay it, get a focus from the side, and nudge it a bit. You try to make the reader forget what you put the man there for. If you say, "I am going to get the ice cream soda," and just go do it, there's no story there. Jack Burden came in there just the way I described. I just can't go shoot him. I've got to stop him. I've got to do something, and so this guy appeared there to stop him. Having him in there filled a dramatic need of fiction, a need of pace. When the novel idea started out some years later, I couldn't do it as a straight dramatic novel. I tried that. I thought on an idle Sunday afternoon: that newspaperman might be useful. The moment of nostalgia might be made into some kind of feeling by which to tell the story. That was how he got in there. I remember that distinctly.

**Mr. Sullivan:** This is wonderful talk, and I certainly don't want to minimize what you and Flannery have said. I think it is absolutely true, but I am speaking among company here which I know perhaps a little more intimately than you. I am afraid we might get a little bit too far off into a romantic notion of the muse.

**Mr. Warren (to Miss O'Connor):** Did you have that in mind?

**Mr. Sullivan:** No, I know you didn't. That's the reason I'm fretting this point so. It seems to me still, that the more you know, the better off you are.

**Miss O'Connor:** When you write the thing through once, you find out what the end is. Then you can go back to the first chapter and put in a lot of those foreshadowings.

**Mr. Warren:** I suppose in another way, Walter, you are raising the question of how does a person sharpen his wits in these matters in order to kill off this *mystique* of writing which I don't think either one of us is trying to promote. But if a person just does ordinary, hard, common sense thinking about writing in general . . . I don't mean about writing only, but about books, novels, poems, stories that he's acquainted with: if he asks himself what he likes or doesn't like about them: that sharpens your wits; it goes deep down into your innards somewhere. It stays there, and is supposed to come out and affect your whole view of things, your whole practice, isn't it?

**Mr. Minetree:** Can you really be that objective about something you're writing?

**Mr. Warren:** I think you have to be at some stage. People are different, you know. Some people pour it out and it is fine; some people pour it out and it's awful. And some people grind it out very hard, and it is awful; and some people grind it out very hard, and it's good. I don't see any generalization. I do think one thing is always true: the degree of self-criticism is only good for a veto. You can throw out what you've got wrong, and you can even try to say why it's wrong, but you can't say, "Now I am going to do it right." At that point you're alone with the alone, and the alone had better come and do it, because you can't. Where the alone happens to be living, I don't know; he's backed up in your nervous system, or a must, or something. You need help at that point. It's got to happen to you, but the way you can make it happen to you, it strikes me, is just by keeping your eyes open about the way the world operates about you, and the way a piece of writing operates that you like or dislike: some know of an awareness as to how they operate. All the critical thinking you can do has to be forgotten as critical thinking whenever you sit down to write. It's bound to affect you, bound to be in you somewhere. Just as everything else is bound to be in you. I'm not disparaging hard critical, or other, thinking, but I think there's a right time and a wrong time for it.

**Mr. Whitehead:** Sir, may I ask a question in two parts? You said that your nostalgic feeling about Burden may have been central. I wonder first, how much of that first chapter, after you had seen it as such, you felt was in a sense the enveloping tone of the novel. It struck me that this is the music that comes before the action in a sense you never forget, and that's in the first chapter. The other part of the question is: were you living in Louisiana when you got that out? from your inside, so to speak.

**Mr. Warren:** I had been living in Louisiana for several years when I started to write. I started the play there, and I finished it in Rome, and then I laid it aside for several years and wrote two other books in between.

**Mr. Whitehead:** It is the man who is the referent, the kicking-off place, not the sense, the sense of the land which you got across in the first chapter.

**Mr. Warren:** No, I can't choose between those two things. It started as the simplest kind of idea. A man who has the gift for power gets his means and his ends mixed up, and gets some power, and there's a backlash on him. He gets killed. It starts with that. Huey Long and Julius Caesar both got killed in the capitol, and there you are. It's as simple as that. It's a germ, an anecdote. And teaching Shakespeare in Louisiana in 1935, you couldn't avoid this speculation.

**Mr. Hoy:** It's appropriate that you should have finished writing the play in Rome.

**Mr. Warren:** Yes. The troops were under the window every day. But the tone of the play had not been the tone of the book. For better or for worse. And the tone of the book turned on the question of getting a lingo for this narrator. I remember that fact quite distinctly. It was a question just of his lingo, and fumbling around with how he's going to talk—he's got to talk some way. A straight journalistic prose would not do. That is the trap of all traps. There has to be an angularity to any piece of writing that claims to have a person behind it. The problem was to find a way for him to talk. It was really a backward process. The character wasn't set up—aside from the lingo, and trying to find a way for him to talk.

**Mr. Whitehead:** Then the man saw that the country existed.

**Mr. Warren:** His ambivalence about what he saw—as a road, as people, as things—was a start. His division of feeling was the way it came out of the start of the lingo. That was the germ. It didn't start with a plot, or conception. This guy gets power, and he gets shot. All the details of Burden's life were improvised. They were improvised in terms of some envisagement of his feelings about everything at the end. But I didn't know what the last chapter was going to be until I got there. I didn't know how I wanted it to feel. Just as Flannery was saying: you go back a little bit, and keep looking back. After you are along the way, keep looking back, and your backward looks along the way will help you go forward. You have to find a logic there that you pursue. If you can't find it, you're in trouble.

**Mr. Harrison:** This may be too broad, but I was reading the other day about a writer who said he was always more optimistic than his writing seemed to be. I find in my own writing, too, that you get a negative issue a lot easier than you get an affirmation in what you are saying. How do you deal with this problem? I have a feeling most writing tends to be more negative than positive at times.

**Mr. Warren (to Miss O'Connor):** Well, you're the one who gets letters from the old lady in California. I don't get them.

**Miss O'Connor:** I don't think about it until I get the letter from the old lady in California. I think when you write a story, you don't say, "This is going to be positive, and this is going to be negative." But I think it is easier to come out with something that is negative because it is just nearer fallen nature. You have to strain yourself for the other, strenuously, too.

**Mr. McNair:** Couldn't you say that it is perhaps more basic—that it goes back actually to the time when a person begins to write. When he begins to write, he is more critical of what he sees about him. Especially you find this in young writers—maybe I shouldn't use that word "young"; I mean in age, anyway, in writing experience. I find that when you look in college publications, you find a great deal of pessimism, and I think perhaps that is caused in part by a certain amount of self-pity on the part of the person. Also, a person in college is re-acting, and perhaps over re-acts over what he has learned, or has been exposed to. And it's decidedly a critical and serious approach that this person takes at this stage of writing, whereas an older writer, writing in *The Saturday Evening Post,* doesn't have nearly those qualities, nor does he write with the seriousness that a person of twenty-two does.

**Miss O'Connor:** If he's writing for *The Saturday Evening Post,* he probably never has.

**Mr. Warren:** I must say that I don't want to nag at a point here that has nothing to do with the one we're discussing, but thinking of oneself as a young writer: it's wrong. I mean, stop boasting. You see, you think you know everything, and you've got to put it down. Don't play yourself for a coward, play for keeps. I think you have to do it that way. Not that nice little exercise I am doing because I am young, and ought to be forgiven. Nothing will be forgiven. It will stink just as much if you did it as if Hemingway did it. It will be just as bad. "I am a young learning writer, and I mean well," is a terrible way to think of it. You're full of urgency and wisdom; you've got to spill it, and set the world aright. A young man I knew some time ago was such a talented young man, really, and so bright. He knew everything. He knew about Kafka and Aristotle; he had read everything. He was the most educated young man I had encountered in years. He was twenty-one years old, a senior at Yale, scholar of the house, prize product of an expensive educational system, and he was leaving his studies, he was so bright. "You just go write a novel or novelette for your project, and no more classes for a year," and things like that. He wrote well; he knew all about how he should feel as a young writer of twenty-one. Like that cartoon I saw in *The New Yorker* some years ago of two little boys reading a book of child care, and one little boy saying, "Jesus, I'm going to be a stinker two years from now." This boy was writing just like that, that kind of self-consciousness, you know. He had dated himself, you see, along the way. He was writing a novel, a love story, and the boy got the girl after certain tribulations that were case book tribulations, it seemed to me, because I am sure he couldn't have gotten them out of real life. Nobody acts like that. They were all so right, intellectually. He knew what people should feel at the age of eighteen, nineteen, twenty, and twenty-one, and fifty-three, and fifty- nine, and seventy-six. He had it all worked out—the life pattern for the fruit fly there at his finger tips. He had a wonderful last paragraph. They got in a clinch and everything was fine, and then they were going to get married. Then this last paragraph: I found it sort of chilling. He said he knew of course this was not really love; he knew that love would come after years of shared experiences: you know, walking the baby with the colic, and the mortgages. Now just imagine a young man twenty-one years old who knows all about Kafka and Aristotle writing like that. The girl ought to run screaming into the brush. He's dated himself as a young writer, you see, a young human being, a post-public adult, some kind of thing like that. His life, everything, was all dated and scaled up. Romeo would never have thought of himself in that way: "This is not true love—that would be seventeen years from now, when we pay off the mortgage." I think it's a dangerous way to look at things. You've got to feel you know the truth, got to tell it—it's the gospel. Hate your elders.

**Mr. Minetree:** What term would you suggest in preference to "young writers"?

**Mr. Warren:** I don't know. That's not my problem.

**Mr. Sullivan:** What do you call yourself, Red?

**Mr. Warren:** I say I am trying to be a writer.

**Mr. Core:** Mr. Warren, how did you finally hit upon the form of *Brother to Dragons*?

**Mr. Warren:** This is awfully like a dissecting room where the corpse is scarcely able to fight back. To answer your question: by fumbling. It started out to be a novel. It clearly couldn't be a novel because the circumstantiality would bog you down, would kill off the main line. And then it started off to be a play. I was doing it in collaboration with a dramatist and producer, and we couldn't quite make it, couldn't agree. I couldn't get a frame for it—the machinery got too much in the way for me. And I was thinking of the wrong kind of problems at the wrong time. But what I was concerned with were the characters, and the emotional sense of it; I didn't want to be bothered by the pacing of it, that technical side. In other words, I didn't naturally think in dramatic terms. The next step was to throw away the notion of the stage play, and keep what was to me the dramatic image, which was the collision of these persons under the unresolved urgency of their earthly experience. All the characters come out of their private purgatory and collide; everybody comes to find out or tell something, rehearse something; it becomes a rehearsal of their unresolved lives in terms of a perspective put on it. That is what the hope was. Then there was the need to tie this to a personal note, putting the writer character in so he could participate in this process, the notion being that we are all unresolved in a way, the dead and the living. This interpenetration, this face of a constant effort to resolve things, came back to the idea of a play again.

**Mr. Mize:** Miss O'Connor, yesterday you spoke about the problem of introducing a definite theological motivation in writing in a society which is somewhat religious only on the surface. Do you think it is possible to write from a definite theological point of view?

**Miss O'Connor:** Yes, if you're a writer in the first place. If you are a writer, you can write from any point of view. I don't think a theological point of view interferes in any way unless it becomes so dominant that you're so full of ideas that you kill the character.

**Mr. Warren:** Flannery, would this be true about theology or anything else: that by the sort of deductive way of going at it— illustrating the point—you're a dead duck before you start?

**Miss O'Connor:** Yes.

**Mr. Whitehead:** If you have faith more or less in your system, then you're kind of proving your system every time you write a story. You go on and write a story, and you look at the story, and you say, "Well look, you haven't fitted to the system—"

**Miss O'Connor:** You don't ever prove anything when you write a story.

**Mr. Whitehead:** Well, you don't prove, but if you begin with a system, you have to be able to see some—

**Miss O'Connor:** You don't begin a story with a system. You can forget about the system. These are things that you believe; they may affect your writing unconsciously. I don't think theology should be a scaffolding.

**Mr. Whitehead:** No, no, I didn't mean it that way. I meant it simply as that which is in your subconscious. You don't have a blueprint. You don't take out the system or diagram, or anything like that. But it's part of your experience, and by virtue of that, is part of you. Your story, drawn from life experience or predicament, will in a sense be quite relative to this, and will be interpreted in terms of that which is subconscious at the end. This is the inevitable situation with all of us, and this gets around the idea of the blueprint approach.

**Mr. Godsey:** Aren't you saying again that the experience or the fable comes before the theme?

**Miss O'Connor:** I don't know. I never think in terms of fable or myth. Those things are far removed from anything that I know when I write.

**Miss Weber:** Miss O'Connor, I was interested in what you said yesterday about the grotesque in fiction writing, particularly in Southern writers. You say that the South can still recognize what a freak is, but perhaps thirty years from now we will be writing about the man in the gray flannel suit. I wondered if you would talk a bit more about that. Perhaps you'd explain why you think that's true.

**Miss O'Connor:** I think as it gets to be more and more city and less country—as we, everything, is reduced to the same flat level—we'll be writing about men in gray flannel suits. That's about all there'll be to write about, I think, as we lose our individuality.

**Mr. Warren:** Did you like *Augie March*?

**Miss O'Connor:** I didn't read it.

**Mr. Warren:** In Bellow's book I had the sense, particularly in the first half, that it was very rich in personalities. An urban, Jewish southside Chicago world, and the people had a lot of bursting-off the page. They were really personalities. They were anything but people in gray flannel suits. That he could in that particular work catch this vigor—this clash—of personality: that's what I liked best about the book.

**Miss O'Connor:** I shouldn't say "city" in that sense. I mean—

**Mr. Warren:** Suburbs, yes.

**Miss O'Connor:** I mean just the proliferation of supermarkets.

**Mr. Warren:** The city has sort of a new romance after the supermarket civilization of the suburbs; it's the new wild west. I think Saul caught that in a way. Certainly there's a richness in his book.

**Miss O'Connor:** That's his region. Everybody has to have a region, and I think in the South we're losing that regional sense.

**Mr. Warren:** Well, you can't keep it for literary purposes.

**Miss O'Connor:** No, because everybody wants the good things of life, like supermarkets—

**Mr. Warren:** —and plastics—

**Miss O'Connor:** —and cellophane. Everybody wants the privilege of being as abstract as the next man.

**Mr. Russell:** We've talked a good bit about this flattening out of personality. For reasons that are undefined to me, I have a good bit more faith in—what do you want to call it—the resilience of individuality, and I think it must find its ways of cropping out between the divisions of the country someway. Do you?

**Mr. Warren:** I think there is danger in our talking about it at all. In a way, as individuals, or as people who live in one place or another place, we can't avoid talking about it, I guess. It's clearly a dehumanizing of man. All the philosophers know about it, and we've heard about it, too. And you see it going on: the draining away of all responsibilities and identities and those things. But it is a little like that scholar of the house, you know: the plan he got from the mental health center, or the university, or wherever he got it, and this is a kind of self-consciousness again. Anybody who sets out to be an individual, a real character, is intolerable. You can't bear the posiness of the crusty old character. "I have a role. I'm going to make my dent on society by having a role. I know my function, my kind of joke, my kind of this, my kind of that." It can run off in that direction. Then you have professional Californians, and all sorts of high-heeled boot boys.

**Mr. Russell:** But they're working at it.

**Mr. Warren:** Everybody is working at it. Every place has its own kind of professional exponents—those who are going to be characters. Characters are the last thing in the world, it seems to me. They're the anti-individuals. They're substituting something for the notion of individuality, for fundamental integrity. We begin to talk about this, and we're singing the swan song. The mere fact that we're talking about it is a danger signal. We're made too self-conscious about it.

**Mr. Whitehead:** I've a feeling that it's an unfortunate thing if some boy in Manhattan hasn't seen a cow or smelled a cedar tree. I'm not quite sure why—

**Mr. Warren:** He feels pretty sorry for you, too.

**Mr. Whitehead:** Yes, I know. That's the thing that bothers me.

**Mr. Warren:** Maybe you're both right.

**Mr. McNair:** I think that what Miss O'Connor and Mr. Warren have been speaking about, this dehumanization, becomes a problem to the writer, because he perhaps is one of the surviving individuals. Perhaps, like Huxley in *Brave New World*, he may write about the whole man, he may write about other individuals, and his dehumanized readers can't even recognize his creation. They can't understand what he's writing about.

**Mr. Warren:** I think maybe we're giving ourselves airs to think we're writing about the whole man.

**Mr. McNair:** Well, comparatively speaking.

**Mr. Warren:** I think it's really what Flannery was talking about yesterday. You write about the whole man, by writing about freaks. If you want to write about the whole man, write with this negative approach. By "freak" I mean anybody you know who is worth writing about.

**Mr. McNair:** You shifted the terms around, but I think you mean the same thing.

**Mr. Warren:** You occasionally get a very complete man, and he has no story. Who cares about Robert E. Lee? Now there's a man who's smooth as an egg. Turn him around, this primordial perfection: you see, he has no story. You can't just say what a wonderful man he was, and that you know he had some chaotic something inside because he's human, but you can't get at it. You know he was probably spoiling with blood lust, otherwise he wouldn't have been in that trade, wouldn't have done so well at it. We can make little schemes like this, and try to jazz it up a bit, but really what you have is this enormous, this monumental self-control, and selflessness, and lots of things like that. You have to improvise a story for him. You don't know his story. It's only the guy who's angular, incomplete, and struggling who has a story. If a person comes out too well, there's not much story. Whoever wants to tell a story of a sainted grandmother, unless you can find some old love letters, and get a new grandfather? In heaven there's no marriage and giving in marriage, and there's no literature.

**Mr. McNair:** Don't you think perhaps it is easier for us in the South to recognize what is important in the freak to be written about.

**Mr. Warren:** We've gotten some good documents.

**Mr. McNair:** Easier for us than for a person in New York, in Manhattan.

**Miss O'Connor:** I don't know. I had a friend from Brooklyn who went out to school in Indiana some place, and he said all he saw out there were healthy blond youngsters. He went back to Brooklyn and he saw a little old man about this high with a cigar in his mouth, and he said "Ah! I'm home."

**Mr. Sullivan:** There's Cheever. He knows some freaks.

**Mr. Warren:** And he knows he knows them. I think his point is, they don't know they're freaks. Until they read his stories about themselves. They think it's the man next door.

**Mr. Whitehead:** In a sense, we're trying to say we can't get too involved in geography. You never know—you make a value judgment on something like that—you speak of something you never have seen—

**Mr. Warren:** I think there's a real problem about your relation to your own world, but I don't think it's a matter of saying what's better and what's worse, because everybody is stuck with his own skin, and his own history, and his own situation. I think he's got every right to think about that, but I don't think it's a matter of choosing up sides for this prupose, this idea that you have to be chosen for this point or that point. I think self-congratulation is a mighty poor way to celebrate human nature. Joyce didn't hang around Dublin pleasing the Dubliners, yet Dublin is always there. Flattering yourself and your community is a mighty poor way, it seems to me, to write anything, or to be a good citizen for that matter. Your own concern is in the defects, the jags.

**Mr. Whitehead:** Yet it's possible you can find a piece of geography which makes you more aware of your own skin.

**Mr. Warren:** You're just stuck with it. You can't choose it.

**Mr. McNair:** That may all be true, and theoretically you can say that a writer in one place will write about the people in his place, bringing out the man in man, as well as the writer in another place.

**Mr. Warren:** He has to.

**Mr. McNair:** But is the best literature written in the South today or not? And why is it best?

**Mr. Warren:** It is not our business to speculate about that point. It's not my business, at least. I am second to no man in admiring a lot of writers that happen to be born in Mississippi and contiguous states, but this sort of speculation doesn't do a writer any good. It leads right away to "Where's my piece of cake?" Something like that. It seems to me it's a very poor way to think about it, unless you want to be a social historian, or a critic, or a literary historian, or something like that. But it's no one's business to think about it very much. To think of how a person is related to his society is a very important point, but I think it should be thought about, not as a writer, but as a person. Thinking about it as a writer is the wrong level for going at it. Any important question should be thought about on its own merits, and not in relation to one as a writer.

**Mr. Boner:** When a writer sits down to write, should he be more conscious of himself as a writer, or as a person.

**Mr. Warren:** He shouldn't be conscious of himself at all. It seems to me he ought to be trying to do his job. A guy learning to catch a baseball has to learn by trial and error. A guy doing a broken field run has to have some training in this. When he's in there he'd better not stop and say, "Am I pretty or not?" When the tackle is bearing down. His business is speed at that point, and nothing but speed— and a little deception.

**Miss Weber:** Miss O'Connor, going back to the business about the grotesque again. I was just wondering how you got hold of the idea of the one-armed carpenter, and the deaf and dumb girl, as a vehicle to tell a story.

**Miss O'Connor:** I don't know. I reckon it just came to me. I did have some trouble with the end of that story. I got it up to his taking the girl away and leaving her. I knew I wanted to do that much, and I did it. But the story wasn't complete. It needed that little boy on the side of the road, and that little boy is really what makes the story work. Of course, I don't know how you get those things. I just waited for it.

**Mr. Whitehead:** Miss O'Connor, you read a lot about the Section Eight School of Southern Writers, and I am kind of following this through in my thinking and reading. I wondered if you are familiar with the work of Carson McCullers?

**Miss O'Connor:** Vaguely.

**Mr. Whitehead:** There are similarities in these things. Even in something like Truman Capote's *Other Voices, Other Rooms*, there's continuity of some sort, and yet there's something that is terribly different.

**Miss O'Connor:** Of course the idiom is alike—the Southern speech. Anybody who picks that up, picks it up. It's what it is. But there are vast differences between—

**Mr. Whitehead:** What you say with it. I mean, there are carnivals all through Southern literature. It's amazing.

**Miss O'Connor:** There are carnivals all over the South. There are evangelists all over the South. I've just had my novel translated into French, and the translator told me he just couldn't set that novel down in France because the French had no idea what an evangelist was. There would have to be some introduction telling them.

**Mr. Whitehead:** Could we possibly say that the difference between these people seeing the same sort of characters is that sub-conscious structure that we don't talk about in the back of their mind, and that this makes the difference with what the characters do in a work?

**Miss O'Connor:** Just different people writing. I'm not Truman Capote, so I don't write like Truman Capote.

**Mr. Whitehead:** Yet somehow people get stuck, get caught in the same basket for good or for ill, usually for ill.

**Mr. Warren:** There's no stupidity it seems to me, at one level, in saying: "All right, there are 'Southern writers' (in quotes,) and start saying what they do share." That is a reasonable thing to say, and a reasonable field of speculation, just so long as you don't equate them. Some clearly are synthetic, and write by imitating, trying to pose as another writer; some are purely imitators and have no personality except a synthetic one they're attached to. They use the group label as a way of trying to achieve some identity, of trying to be writers at all. But that is universally a problem; he's got to learn from somebody else. It is very hard for him to find any kind of voice of his own. That's his big trouble, it seems to me. But he can't find it except by saying he's going to find it, he's got to work around the problem, not head on into it. If he heads on into it, he's probably going to be the worst kind of imitator. Or he'll invent something to get a difference. But I don't see anything reprehensible in grouping a whole lot of—no use naming names, you know all the names—just say the "Southern writers." They do share something; what they do with what they share is a very important thing; what they are from one to another is a very important difference. That is what makes the fact that you can group them together a rather piquant thing. If you look at the next step, an ordinary writer on the subject says what they share, and then makes the group. The interesting thing is, having made the groups, seeing then what the differences are within that, in terms of all sorts of things: kinds of talents, temperaments, philosophy, and god knows what. But that is the next stage, and it's rarely done.

**Mr. Sullivan:** There seems to be some sort of tacit agreement here that the South is a rich land of images. Could you say something about the dangers of this attitude of not transcending the image. It seems to me that the great danger there is that the Southern writer will be so busy being Southern that he won't be anything else.

**Mr. Warren:** It's certainly a trap.

**Mr. Sullivan:** Do you think it's as great a trap as I seem to think it is?

**Mr. Warren:** Well, it couldn't be worse.

**Mr. Sullivan:** How about that, Flannery?

**Miss O'Connor:** I don't know. I think if you're a real writer, you can avoid that kind of thing. There are so many horrible examples of regional writers, and the South is loaded. There's one behind every bush. So many awful examples. It's the first thing you think of avoiding.

**Mr. Warren:** Yet you're stuck with your own experiences, your own world around you.

**Miss O'Connor:** You have to keep going in deeper.

# An Afternoon with Flannery O'Connor
Betsy Lochridge/October 1959

From *The Atlanta Journal and Constitution Magazine,* 1 November 1959, 38-40. © 1959 The Atlanta Journal and Constitution. Reprinted by permission.

"Don't make me out a farm girl," says Flannery O'Connor. "All I know about the land is, it's underneath me."

The 34-year old author, who has in 10 years earned a reputation as one of this country's outstanding fiction artists, lives quietly with her mother in a rambling white farmhouse near Milledgeville.

Here, in a pleasant downstairs bedroom, she finished her first novel, *Wise Blood,* and a collection of short stories, *A Good Man Is Hard to Find.* Her forthcoming novel, *The Violent Bear It Away,* due for February publication by Farrar, Straus & Cudahy, was written here. So were the short stories which have earned her three O. Henry awards, two Kenyon fellowships, a grant from the National Institute of Arts and Letters and a Ford Foundation grant under which she is now working.

Born in Savannah, Miss O'Connor is one Southern writer who believes that "Southern writers are stuck with the South, and it's a very good thing to be stuck with."

Except for a year of graduate work at the University of Iowa, and a short stint in New York City, she has spent her life in the South. She attended Savannah parochial schools, Milledgeville High School and graduated from Georgia State College for Women.

Her drawl is frankly Southern. Her manner is quiet, unassuming yet assured, and sparked with humor. Her face is strong, full and sensitive. Her dark eyes are sharply observant—her paintings of churches and farm scenes, which line the dining room of the farmhouse, testify to how much and how well she sees. Her surroundings are indicative of her taste for the simple, the pleasant and the unpretentious. There is no foolishness about her.

"People seem to surround being-a-writer with a kind of false mystique, as if what is required to be a writer is a writer's temperament," she says. "Most of the people I know with writers' temperaments aren't doing any writing."

Miss O'Connor is writing steadily three hours a day, regardless of her mood. "If I waited for inspiration, I'd still be waiting," she says.

Her mother runs the farm. "I don't do anything around here besides write except occasionally I might pick up an egg or something," she says.

When her morning's writing is done, she settles into a rocker on the front porch and just looks.

The view is sweeping, the perspective wide. There is a blue haze of hills in the distance; to the right are broad pastures grazed by calves and a meditative bull. Fields gilded with goldenrod slope down to a dazzling pond. Peacocks sweep majestically through the front yard and pea fowl and Chinese geese stalk the paths among tangles of morning glories, and casual rows of zinnias and tiger lilies.

Flannery's avocation is chickens. "When I was six I had a chicken that walked backward and was in the Pathe News. I was in it too with the chicken. I was just there to assist the chicken but it was the high point in my life. Everything since has been anticlimax."

The humor which flavors her conversation also colors her work. A rare humor, it is based on an understanding of human nature and a strong sense of the ridiculous, the tragic and the ironic. She is seldom deceived, nor is the reader.

"Mine is a comic art," she says, "but that does not detract from its seriousness."

Devoutly Catholic, she infuses her work with a sense of mystery, an extra dimension which gives her fiction a quality of timelessness.

Her faith furnishes her with "a sense of continuity from the time of Christ," she says. "I can accept the universe as it is—I don't have to make up my own sense of values; I can apply to a judgment higher than my own—I'm not limited to what I personally feel or think. And I have a sense of personal responsibility; I believe that a person is always valuable and always responsible."

Miss O'Connor is not at all concerned with markets or trends, with what will sell or what is popular.

Doesn't she want readers?

"I can wait," she says. "A few readers go a long way when they're the right kind. There are so many of the other kind. The writer is only free when he can tell the reader to go jump in the lake. You want, of course, to get what you have to show across to him, but whether he likes it or not is no concern of the writer."

Whom does she try to please?

"I try to satisfy those necessities that make themselves felt in the work itself. When I write, I am a maker. I think about what I am making. St. Thomas called art reason in making. When I write I feel I am engaged in the reasonable use of the unreasonable. In art the reason goes wherever the imagination goes. We have reduced the uses of reason terribly. You say a thing is reasonable and people think you mean it's safe. What's reasonable is seldom safe and always exciting."

Unlike many writers, Miss O'Connor enjoys the actual writing. She works on a typewriter, turns out about three pages a day—"but I may tear it all to pieces the next day.

"It is well to look at your own work with an objective eye, as if someone else had written it. When I have finished a story, I enjoy reading it. If I don't enjoy reading it, then it is not finished."

*The Violent Bear It Away* was seven years in the writing. The novel will speak for itself; she doesn't like to talk about it.

"One reason I like to publish short stories is that nobody pays any attention to them," she says. "In 10 years or so they begin to be known but the process has not been obnoxious. When you publish a novel, the racket is like a fox in the hen house."

She thinks it not at all unusual that a literary reputation should be forged on an isolated Georgia farm.

"All writers are local somewhere," she says simply. "And writers thrive on isolation."

Though far removed from any literary circles, she maintains a full creative life. There are books—Joseph Conrad is her favorite author. There is her correspondence with other writers—Caroline Gordon, Robie McCauley and Robert Fitzgerald. There are the Wednesday night gatherings when friends from Milledgeville ride out to spend the evening reading aloud and talking on the O'Connors' spacious screened porch. And there are occasional visits from other writers, most of them young like herself, and like herself, Southern in background.

She believes the best writing today is being done in the South. One reason she cites is that this is the Bible belt. "The Bible makes the absolute concrete; the story writer also tries to make something concrete."

She believes that, to her own fiction, the South has contributed "its idiom and its rich and strained social setup."

"The South," she says, blossoms with every kind of complication and contradiction. I see a good many young writers, Southerners, who think that the first thing they had better do in order to write well is not to use characters who are obviously Southern and who speak our idiom. They feel that if they do they will be regional writers. But the fact is that you can't cut a character off from his society and say much about him as an individual. We carry our history and our beliefs and customs and vices and virtues around in our idiom. You can't say anything significant about the mystery of a personality unless you put that personality in a social context that belongs to it."

From the beginning, her stories about the South have found a market. As a writer, she counts herself extremely fortunate. "Most writers have many obstacles put in their way. I have had none," she says, characteristically discounting the crippling disease which limits her activities and makes crutches a necessity.

"There has been no interesting or noble struggle. The only thing I wrestle with is the language, and a certain poverty of means in handling it, but this is merely what you have to do to write at all."

# Visit to Flannery O'Connor Proves a Novel Experience

Margaret Turner/May 1960

From *The Atlanta Journal and Constitution,* 29 May 1960, sec. G, 2. © 1960 The Atlanta Journal and Constitution. Reprinted by permission.

Strutting peacocks and honking geese gave us a warm but boisterous welcome as we drove up the driveway to the rambling farmhouse where author Flannery O'Connor lives.

A group of Theta Sigma Phi's, National Fraternity for Women in Journalism, had been invited to Flannery's for tea. We found her home just outside Milledgeville the kind of place we expected to see. Old boxwood and a bed of hollyhocks leaning toward the afternoon sun gave it unmistakable Southern charm.

The 34-year-old author was the recipient of the Theta Sigma Phi annual Brenda award, presented by proxy at the organization's Matrix Table in April. And the group invited to tea delivered the golden Brenda statue to her in person.

Meeting Flannery was like renewing ties with an old acquaintance, we had learned so much about her from the many feature stories and book reviews on her work. She is a quiet person except when she has something to say, and what she says is generally to the point and often spiked with dry humor. She's not prone to indulge in idle chatter.

The group sat in a circle on the wide verandah which boasts a sweeping view of distant hills. At the far end there was an old-fashioned hammock which beckoned, but we preferred to sit and talk.

We discussed many things—Flannery's hobbies, which are raising peacocks and Chinese geese "because they're no trouble at all," and painting life on the farm.

We talked about the 150-year-old farmhouse in which the author

41

and her mother, Mrs. Edward F. O'Connor, have made their home
since 1950. Mrs. O'Connor, with the help of a displaced Polish
family, runs a dairy farm there.

The mother and daughter formerly lived in Mrs. O'Connor's
ancestral home in Milledgeville. Now occupied by Flannery's aunt,
Mary Cline, the antebellum house, filled with antiques, is a favorite
on Milledgeville's home and garden tours. It once served as the
governor's mansion in the 1830s during the time the new governor's
mansion was being built. (Milledgeville was the state capital before it
was moved to Atlanta in 1868.)

We finally got around to the subject of writing.

According to critics, Flannery writes better than nearly anybody
else now living. Her writing has been compared to the works of
Tennessee Williams, William Faulkner and the Russian novelist and
short-story writer Dostoyevsky. All are distinguished by their character
studies which are in the realm of abnormal psychology.

Flannery's writings have won three O'Henry awards, two Kenyon
Fellowships, a Ford Foundation grant and a grant from the National
Institute of Arts and Letters. Her two novels are *Wise Blood* and *The
Violent Bear It Away.* The best known of her works is her book of
short stories, *A Good Man is Hard to Find.*

Asked if her characters are drawn from real life, the author said
that if she had known too many of the people she writes about she
might not be around to write about them.

"The imagination works on what the eye sees, but it molds and
directs this to the end of whatever it is making," she explained. "So
my characters are both and at the same time drawn from life and
entirely imaginary. Not too many people claim to see themselves in
them."

She prefers to call her work "grotesque," meaning that she does
not write in a naturalistic vein but uses distortion to make what is not
readily observable more observable.

Why, we ventured to ask, does a writer of fiction feel that he has to
shock to get through to the average reader?

"Not every writer of fiction feels that he has to shock to get through
to the average reader," she said. "I believe that the 'average' reader,
however, is a good deal below average. People say with considerable

satisfaction, 'Oh, I'm an average reader,' when the fact is they never learned to read in the first place, and probably never will.

"You see people who are supposed to be highly educated who don't know trashy fiction from any other kind," she continued. "If you have the values of your time, you can usually write without having to shock anyone to attention; but if you want to show something that the majority don't believe in or wish to see, then you have to get and hold their attention usually by extreme means."

Some folks say that writers are born, not made, and that courses in writing techniques seldom help. We asked Flannery about this, knowing she had studied the novel at the University of Iowa.

"'I' ters are born but they have to be nourished," she pointed out. ıechnique is not something you learn and apply to what you have to do; it is a way of making something, that grows naturally out of what you have to say and show, and it is different for every piece of work."

She thinks that writing education should go along with the general education, that it should start in the first grade and continue as long as the school system has the pupil in its clutches.

"Everywhere I go I'm asked if I think universities stifle writers," she said. "I think they don't stifle enough of them. The kind of writing that can be taught is the kind you then have to teach people not to read. . . ."

She explained that what she had at the University of Iowa was valuable, "but it wasn't training to write as such; it was training to read with critical attention—my own work and other people's."

As for Flannery's crippling disease which requires the use of crutches, she said "the disease is of no consequence to my writing, since for that I use my head and not my feet."

# She Writes Powerful Fiction
Robert Donner [Richard Gilman]/September 1960

From *The Sign,* 40 (March 1961), 46-48. Reprinted by permission of Richard Gilman.

Milledgeville, Georgia, is a quiet town of some 10,000 inhabitants which lies about a hundred miles from Atlanta, whose predecessor as the state capital it was before the Civil War. Among its other distinctions, one might mention the fact that it was the birthplace of Oliver Hardy, of Laurel and Hardy fame, and that among its current residents is Mrs. Barbara Powers, the wife of the U-2 pilot who was shot down last spring over Russia and convicted of espionage.

When I was there last fall, Milledgeville was being visited by several reporters seeking interviews with Mrs. Powers, who had just returned from Moscow. My own purpose in coming, however, was quite different. I had come to see Flannery O'Connor, one of the most highly regarded of younger American writers.

Her short stories and novels have been receiving increasing praise from critics and readers both in this country and abroad. One English writer has called her the most impressive talent America has produced since the war, while an American critic, Granville Hicks, has said, "If there is a young writer who has given clearer evidence of originality and power than Flannery O'Connor, I cannot think who it is."

For commentators such as these, as well as for the small but dedicated public that admires her work (she is by no means a "popular" writer), what stands out in Miss O'Connor's writing is its moral quality, wedded to a high order of imagination. For the people she writes about—poor, rural Southern Protestants mostly—are caught up in situations of spiritual conflict that point to something much wider than themselves: they are universal dramas that we all participate in. Love and lovelessness, community and loneliness, faith and despair—these are the poles of her art, as they are the poles between which all of us lead our lives.

Yet there is nothing sermon-like about these stories. Miss O'Connor is concerned in her vocation as an artist to render life as she sees it, with exact truth, leaving the *explicit* moral and theological lessons to be drawn by those whose function it is. The way she approaches life is deeply shaped by her Catholic faith, however. As she says, "The Catholic writer, in so far as he has the mind of the Church, will feel life from the standpoint of the central Christian mystery: that it has for all its horror, been found by God to be worth dying for."

For various reasons—among them the fact that she lives far from any center of cultural activity, that her work differs in its underlying religious vision from that of most of her contemporaries, and that she has a painful illness that requires her to go about on crutches—a legend to the effect that she is a recluse, living in complete isolation, has grown up around Flannery O'Connor.

Even before I met her I learned that this picture was thoroughly distorted. Riding on the bus from Atlanta through the red-clay country of central Georgia, I fell into conversation with a young man who had noticed that I was reading *Wise Blood,* Miss O'Connor's first novel. He was a student at the University of Chicago, on his way home from the summer session, and he told me that he was well acquainted with the writer and that her home was the scene of frequent gatherings in which lively conversations on life and literature took place. "Oh, no," he said, as our bus pulled in, "she's certainly not a hermit, though she's not an extrovert either."

Miss O'Connor was waiting for me in a car driven by her mother. A brown-haired, slender woman in her thirties, she greeted me warmly, speaking in a soft voice with a medium-rich Southern accent. Before we went to their farm home, a few miles outside of Milledgeville, the O'Connors showed me the town—the old, pillared mansions along the wide residential streets, the red-stone buildings of the Georgia State College for Women, which Miss O'Connor had attended, the crumbling one-time governor's mansion now occupied by the

president of the college, the little Church of the Sacred Heart where
Milledgeville's Catholics worship. Then we drove the short and
pleasant ride out to the farm.

I had read that Miss O'Connor raised peacocks as a hobby, and
indeed there they were, strutting around the main house in lordly
possession, although it wasn't the season for their splendid tails to be
in bloom. "I like having them around," Miss O'Connor said, as we
sat on the steps in the late afternoon sunshine and fed a hen and her
five brown chicks from a can of dried corn kernels, chatting at
random while Mrs. O'Connor prepared dinner.

Later we sat on rocking-chairs on the porch while night insects
fluttered against the screens and the sound of some animal could be
heard occasionally from the darkness outside. I asked Miss O'Connor
for a brief autobiographical sketch, which she readily gave me,
though I could see that her modesty and reticence made it something
of a chore for her to talk about herself.

She was born March 25, 1925, in Savannah, where her father was
in the real estate business ("there aren't any artists in my
background"). Later he became an appraiser for the FHA and in 1938
the family moved to Milledgeville, which was Mrs. O'Connor's home
town. Flannery (she was christened *Mary* Flannery, dropping the first
name when she began to publish, though her friends and relatives
still use it) attended Peabody High School and in 1942 entered
Georgia State College for Women, earning her degree in three years
under the accelerated wartime curriculum.

She had majored in the social sciences and had thought of
becoming a teacher ("I'm rather glad things didn't work out that
way"), but after her graduation she was granted a fellowship at the
University of Iowa and began to write. Her first published story
appeared in the literary magazine *Accent* in 1946 and from then on
her career progressed steadily.

Her first novel *Wise Blood* (a bizarre, savagely funny, and deeply
felt story about a young religious fanatic) was begun in 1948, the
year she left Iowa, and published in 1951. Its final pages were
composed under trying circumstances, for in the spring of 1951,
while she was staying with friends in Connecticut, she suffered a
severe attack of *lupus*, a disease of the rheumatic order, and had
literally to sweat out every word as she put it on paper.

Since then she has been on cortisone, which keeps the malady in check, though there is no known cure. She returned to Milledgeville, where her mother had purchased a farm (her father had died in 1941), and has lived there ever since, writing and publishing regularly. From my own knowledge I filled in the rest of her biography.

Ten of her stories were published in 1955 under the title of *A Good Man is Hard to Find,* and her second novel, *The Violent Bear it Away,* a powerful story of a youth caught between the life of reason and that of prophecy, appeared early this year. Her stories have earned several important literary awards, including the O. Henry prize, and she had been the recipient of grants from both the National Academy of Arts and Letters and the Ford Foundation.

When she was describing her illness to me, her tone was remarkably matter-of-fact, without a trace of self-pity. And I discovered that, while the disease naturally limits her movements, it hasn't kept her rooted to one spot. She has participated in a number of writers' conferences and given readings at colleges as far north as Minnesota (where she recently read her work to the students at the College of St. Catherine in St. Paul). In 1957 she traveled to Lourdes on a pilgrimage with her mother and a party of townspeople.

When we began to talk about her work itself, she became much more animated, although she retained that note of half-humorous detachment I had observed before. "I don't have any theory of literature," she said. "I simply keep doing things the wrong way over and over until they suddenly come out right . . . That's one reason why I'm such a slow worker. *The Violent Bear it Away* took me seven years to write—of course I did other things from time to time—and I can't seem to turn out more than two stories a year. I have to have a "story" in mind—some incident or observation that excites me and in which I see fictional possibilities—before I can start a formal piece. But I do try to write at least three hours every morning, since discipline is so important."

She doesn't read many novels, she said, nor is she much of a reader in general. Among her favorite authors are Dostoievsky and Hawthorne, and she returns to them at regular intervals. Of the books she does read, many come to her from the Atlanta diocesan paper, for which she reviews frequently.

We discussed the reactions to her work among different kinds of readers. One that continually surprised her, she said, was the occasional charge that her stories lacked compassion for their characters. I suggested that this stemmed from the difficulty some people had in accepting a vision of humanity in its true behavior, with its passions, prejudices, conflicts, hungers, and secret dreams revealed to the eye, and with no explicit "uplifting" or consoling message to ease the shock. The humor in her writing was enough, it seemed to me, to demonstrate that her work was far from being deficient in sympathy and love.

More than that, a true Christian sense of existence is at the center of her work. What has made her a thorny writer for some readers is that her optimism is not on the surface. She had written once, "If the Catholic writer hopes to reveal mysteries, he will have to do it by describing truthfully what he sees from where he is. A purely affirmative vision cannot be demanded of him without limiting his freedom to observe what man has done with the things of God."

And I reflected on some of her stories: how behind the cruel, sardonic, often terrifying events that take place in them there is a hidden radiance, a light made up of hope and faith in ultimate salvation, and hope and faith in mankind, struggling, involved in evil, seeking to extricate itself, falling back and rising again.

But to be misunderstood is the frequent fate of writers. Miss O'Connor told me an amusing anecdote in illustration. One of her stories had been sold to television. When finally presented it had been turned upside down—a pointed, ironical tale of avarice, betrayal, and the birth of moral insight having become a piece of sentimental, easy-to-take escapism. The morning after the telecast, she was approached in town by an acquaintance who had never before indicated the slightest awareness of Miss O'Connor's stature as an artist. "Why, Mary Flannery," the woman said to her, "I do declare, I never dreamed you could do such nice work."

It was getting late. We rose and Miss O'Connor started checking the double locks on both the front and rear doors. When I asked her why all the precautions, she said, "Well, on one side of town there's the largest insane asylum in the world and on the other a home for delinquent boys. So we have to be careful about uninvited guests."

As I was going upstairs, she called after me, "Don't be alarmed if you hear something that sounds like 'Help!' It's only the peacocks." Nevertheless I was pretty badly shaken when I did hear it, just before I fell asleep.

After breakfast the next day, we took a tour of the farm. It's an impressive one, 1,700 acres stretching over hilly countryside and including pasture-land for a herd of a hundred cattle and the shetland ponies which are raised as a sideline, and an extensive stand of timber. As we rode across the fields to visit the ponies grazing among shrubs and small trees in a corner of the pasture, Flannery's mother explained that she had recently sold the timber rights to her trees to a lumber company, the buzzing of whose saws we could hear across the blue, hazy air.

The writer's mother, incidentally, struck me as an amazingly competent woman, of a pioneer-like stamina and courage. Though she employs a Polish refugee family and several Negro laborers to run the place, it was clear that the reins of the complex operation were in her hands.

Back in the house again, Miss O'Connor and I settled down to more conversation. I wanted to know about her family's roots in the area, and she told me that her great-grandfather had settled in Milledgeville around the time of the Civil War. It was her great-grandmother who had had the Catholic Church built: before that, Mass for the few local Catholics had been celebrated in her parlor by a visiting priest. Today there are about two hundred Catholic families and, Miss O'Connor commented, they get along amiably enough with their Protestant neighbors.

From this we passed to a discussion of the phenomenon of Southern writers, who occupy so large a position in American literature. "I think it's because the Southerner possesses a story-telling tradition" Miss O'Connor said. "When a Southerner wants to make a point, he tells a story; it's actually his way of reasoning and dealing with experience." The South, she added, while changing rapidly, was still largely rural and its people were therefore closer to the land and to the legends and myths which spring from it.

I reflected that the people in her stories possessed that earthiness and quality of permanence she was describing, and that her humility as a writer lay in her willingness to write about them and to find in their lives the material for her art, even though they were not on the surface what we think of as "representative" or typical.

A few days after my visit, I looked up the scattered writings of Flannery O'Connor that I hadn't yet read. In an essay called "The Church and the Fiction-Writer," which had appeared in *America*, I came upon a passage that perfectly expressed her credo as a creative writer. "What the fiction writer will discover," she had written, ". . . is that he cannot move or mold reality in the interests of abstract truth. The writer learns, perhaps more quickly than the reader, to be humble in the face of what is."

# On Flannery O'Connor
Richard Gilman/September 1960

From *The New York Review of Books*, 21 August 1969, 24-26.
© 1969 The New York Review of Books. Reprinted by permission. Review of *Mystery and Manners*.

I first came to know Flannery O'Connor through a shy little note of thanks she sent me for some words of praise I had written about her first book of stories, *A Good Man Is Hard to Find,* in an obscure Catholic magazine called *Jubilee.* I remember that I described the stories as strange, brilliant, wholly original, and also that I resolutely kept from discussing them in any "Catholic" perspective. She was especially grateful for that, she told me later when we had become friends. It wasn't that she thought there shouldn't be a Catholic perspective on her work—far from it—but that such a procedure ought to wait until her art was secure, as art. It was extremely important to her that her writing be seen as independent, particularly from any expectations about its moral or spiritual testimony.

Throughout her life she was caught in the various pressures of our tendency to classify and sociologize art, our impatience with art as itself. ("All I mean by art," she wrote in one of the essays and talks which her good friends Sally and Robert Fitzgerald have collected in this volume, "is writing something that is valuable in itself and that works in itself.") An intense, unapologetic, and unshakable Catholic, she was for most Catholics who were at all aware of her an agent of something inimical to faith and fatal to moral equilibrium; for a more sophisticated minority she was a writer of splendor and revelation, which were however often seen more as spiritual than as aesthetic. Besides this, she suffered from being categorized by place and theme: a "Southern" writer, a writer of the "grotesque." As she wrote in an essay reprinted here, "even if there are no genuine schools in American letters today, there is always some critic who has just invented one and who is ready to put you into it."

Against this tendency there was the temptation to see her as wholly strange, an unfathomable eccentric who sent off her dark comic tales from the isolation of her Georgia farm, where she remained entirely outside the gossip, the play of personality, of the literary world, and had no part in its economy or politics. I remember how, before I knew her, the reports of her illness—that she was the victim of some mysterious disease which compelled her to go about on crutches— added to her disturbing, unaccountable aura, and how unsettling it had been to find out earlier, as I did only after having read several of her stories, that she wasn't a man. (When I visited her later I found it hard to get used to her mother's calling "*Mary* Flannery"; she had dropped the first name because, as she told me, "who was likely to buy the stories of an Irish washerwoman?")

After my reply to her note we corresponded at long intervals, mostly Christmas cards and an occasional postcard of mine to her from Europe or Mexico and of hers to me from the farm, one of them with a photograph of peacocks on it. Then in the fall of 1960 I wrote her that I was going to be in the South on a trip, and could I come to see her? She'd be delighted, she said, and sent instructions on how to get from Atlanta to Milledgeville, some hundred miles downstate.

Flannery and her mother, Regina, a formidable looking woman whom I judged to be about sixty, met me at the bus station in their car, which Mrs. O'Connor drove, while Flannery sat in the back, her crutches resting against the seat alongside her. "I expect you'll want a shower," was the first thing she said to me. It had been a hot afternoon and the bus hadn't been air-conditioned. I told her I would and climbed in front. We drove through the town, which had been the state capitol for a time after the Civil War and was the home of the Georgia State College for Women, the school Flannery had gone to.

She conducted the drive as a mock exercise in Southern pride of place. "There's one of the real famous gardens round here," she said once, and later, "that place with the decadent columns is where our second most distinguished citizen lives." The big-porched, wide-pillared house turned out to be the home of Carl Vinson, the long-time chairman of the House Military Affairs Committee. Then we came to a house with an even bigger porch and pillars and Flannery said, her tone shifting to affection, "and that was the house of our

*most* distinguished citizen." It was the boyhood home of Oliver
Hardy, who, Mrs. O'Connor remembered, used to sit and rock
alongside his mother on the porch, a great rotund youth who was
gathering energy to pick himself up and go star in Hollywood.

The farm was much bigger than I'd expected, an expanse of
planted fields with a stretch of timberland beyond. Mrs. O'Connor
was engaged just then in selling some trees for lumber—"I don't
know how we're going to keep this place up, with no help you can
depend on and nothing coming in," she said in what seemed a
strangely aggressive apology—and throughout my stay I could hear
the dull whine of distant buzz-saws.

After my shower I joined Flannery at the side door of the rather
nondescript white farmhouse, where she was sitting feeding her
peafowl. She handed me the can filled with dried corn kernels and I
gingerly held them out to the birds, which were not in feather then,
being instead rather scruffy-looking, dirty-brown creatures. (There is
a splendid account, with the flavor of one of Lawrence's essays, of
her feelings and ideas about peacocks, which appeared in *Holiday* in
1961 and is reprinted in this collection.)

There, with the sun going down and the birds coming jerkily and
indifferently up to be fed, we began to talk, and became so
engrossed in it that Mrs. O'Connor, of whose martinet qualities I was
to have further experience, had to shout more and more vehemently
when dinner was ready. It was a conversation that ranged over
religion, American life, ourselves, and, especially, literature, and it
was to go on with only the most necessary interruptions for the entire
three days I was there.

I realize that I have not yet described her, and this delay is true to
what happened that day. Before I met her I had found out something
about her illness. She was suffering from lupus, a terrifying disease
related to arthritis, which generally attacks the blood vessels and of
which her father had died in his early forties. I had known she was
crippled and that the disease had distorted her face, but the only
picture of her I had seen had been on the back of *Wise Blood* and
been taken before the illness broke out.

Knowing what I did, I had held off looking at her from the moment
of my arrival. Uncertain and afraid of what I might feel, self-conscious
and ashamed of it, I had found myself glancing past her face, averting

my eyes when she moved laboriously about, not wanting yet to see her. But then, as we talked, something broke and I was looking at her, at her face twisted to one side, at her stiff and somewhat puffy hands and arms, and at her thinning and lusterless hair. From then on, although I would be shaken by an occasional spasm of pity I hated feeling, her appearance was absorbed for me into her presence and—I don't use the word lightly—transfigured by it.

Tough-minded, laconic, with a marvelous wit and an absolute absence of self-pity, she made me understand, as never before or since, what spiritual heroism and beauty can be. There was nothing soft in it, no "radiance," no conventional serenity. She could be cutting, as in her remarks about certain writers she thought were frauds or about the kinds of stupidity she encountered in some of her admirers. She could exhibit impatience, doubt, pleasure in compliments, great distress at unfavorable reviews. But she was almost entirely free from calculation, from concern with what might be expected of her, and from any desire to question her fate or move into outrage.

She went to mass every day, said grace, and wasn't ashamed of saying "Our Lady." But as she writes in a number of essays in this book, her Catholicism was mainly a matter of belief in mysteries and in the perilous balance between grace and the despoliation of the self. She was the furthest thing from a moralist; I never heard her make a moral judgment that wasn't first or at the same time a philosophic or an aesthetic one.

She was extremely firm in almost all her judgments and possessed nothing of what we like to call an "inquiring" mind. But this wasn't the consequence of her Catholicism or of her being Southern, as some unsympathetic critics have argued. Being with her I had the feeling that just as her fiction cost some effort to go beyond its immediate exotic data, its local colorations, and apparently perverse violence, so she had to be seen as only tactically "narrow" or unsophisticated. For one thing, her illness had put her against the wall, so that being interested in anything that wasn't fiercely to her purpose in the small space she had to operate in was a rare luxury. Beyond this, she wasn't being called upon to "know" anything; she was an artist, and I think she was right in what she wrote in "The Nature and Aim of Fiction," reprinted here: "there's a certain grain of

stupidity that the writer of fiction can hardly do without, and this is
the quality of having to stare, of not getting the point at once." To
write is to sacrifice what you think you know.

She suspected that she didn't know the intellectual world, and was
aware that it had its suspicions of her. She wasn't, of course, wholly
the product of small-time and rural education and experience; she
had attended the University of Iowa's Writer's Workshop, had spent
some time in the East before her illness with her friends the
Fitzgeralds, and was in touch with other writer-friends through
correspondence and occasional visits. Until the last stages of her
illness she made one or two trips a year to talk at colleges or
conferences. Yet I wasn't surprised when she asked me if I thought
she had "gotten right" the intellectual (Rayber, the teacher) in *The
Violent Bear it Away*. "I don't reckon he'd be very convincing to you
folks in New York," she said. I said, after wondering for a moment
where I stood, no, he wasn't a very convincing intellectual and,
growing bolder, that in fact I thought he was one of the few occasions
when her art failed because she hadn't sacrificed what she thought
she knew. She was silent and then said she thought I was probably
right, and I could feel our connection deepening from this point.

I have said that she didn't have an inquiring mind, yet one thing
she wanted to know was what I thought about the way certain writers
acted and lived. She was especially interested in Norman Mailer. "I
just can't understand why he doesn't let his work speak for itself,"
she said, "doesn't he think it would?" Then she added, "Why does
he always push forward and make such a spectacle of himself?" I told
her that I thought that this had to do with a conflict between art and
life, or contemplation and action, and that in general Jewish writers,
for all sorts of social and psychic reasons, found it difficult to
disappear behind their work. She greeted my comments with little
nods and a shake or two of her head, as though something she'd
found puzzling had at last been given clear expression, if not
explained.

From time to time we talked about the South, both in its own right
and as it offered itself for her work. (Many of the things she said can
be found in this collection.) If she disliked being known as a Southern
writer, it wasn't because she thought there was any loss or injury in
being one—quite the contrary—but for the same reason she didn't

South fed her, it was a "story-telling" region, and she believed, too, that, decaying and even vicious as its manners were, they were still manners, ways of ordering and identifying relationships that the North, with its "abstract" life, lacked, and greatly useful for the writer of fiction.

But she thought herself in no sense a regionalist and had contempt for the kind of Southern writer—Carson McCullers was one she mentioned—who she thought exploited the South, rested on its easier legends, its "color" and sentimental view of itself. Faulkner she greatly admired; he had set limits and defined possibilities for any writer's use of the region, but his work wasn't anything you'd want your own to resemble. "After all," she said, "nobody wants his mule and wagon stalled on the same track the Dixie Limited is roaring down." (The remark is to be found in one of the pieces in this book, a talk on Southern writing, which an editor's note says she gave at a Georgia women's college a month after I was with her. She knew a good thing when she heard it.)

All around us I saw the material of her fiction, the South she used: the leathery, taciturn country people, the hired hands, the mythical elderly ladies we met in town, the dirt roads, the pick-up trucks, Dr. Pepper signs, pentecostal churches. Most central of all was her mother, who enters into so many of her stories as the fulcrum of their violent moral action. There was something larger than life about her, which came, I realized, from her having already been transformed in my consciousness into the bearer of aesthetic news. Actually, she was a small, intense, enormously efficient woman, who, as she fussed strenuously and even tyrannically over Flannery, gave off an air of martyrdom which was the exact opposite of her daughter's quiet acceptance.

One evening at dinner she said to me, while Flannery stared at her food in embarrassment, "now I want you to tell me what's wrong with those publishers up there in New York. Do you know know many copies of Mary Flannery's novel have been sold? Three thousand two hundred and seventy eight, that's how many copies of Mary Flannery's novel have been sold, and there is something very wrong with that, they are not doing right by her." I said that Farrar, Straus was a fine publisher and that The Violent Bear It Away wasn't the kind of novel likely to have a big sale. And then I added that

Flannery's reputation was more and more secure and that was the
important thing. "Important thing!" she snorted, "reputations don't
buy groceries."

I tell this incident because it seemed to me that what it represented
was another of the pressures that Flannery O'Connor lived through
and in the face of which made her art. No writer I've known had such
devotion to art, felt so much a conduit rather than a source, expected
so little beyond internal satisfactions. Something she wrote in an
essay reprinted here seems to me to convey an essential quality of
her lonely, besieged, and unnoticed life and to be a motto for the
risks she took and the things she made: "The writer has no rights
except those he forges for himself within his own work."

We said goodby at the bus station, Mrs. O'Connor calling after me
an invitation to come back to Andalusia, as the farm was called,
whenever I found myself in Georgia, Flannery leaning over with
difficulty to wave from the car window. I didn't see her again. We
corresponded, again sporadically, the last note I had from her coming
a few months before she died. She would almost never fail to pay me
some little compliment on things I'd written and encourage me in
what I hoped to write. I felt unequal to encouraging her; all I could
hope to do, and I know I never succeeded, was to try to make her
know how much understanding of courage she had made it possible
for me to have.

# An Interview with Flannery O'Connor

Katherine Fugin, Faye Rivard, and Margaret Sieh/October 1960

From *Censer* [College of St. Teresa, Winona, MN], Fall 1960, 28-30. Reprinted by permission.

Flannery O'Connor, author of *The Violent Bear It Away* and *A Good Man Is Hard to Find*, was a guest lecturer at the College of Saint Teresa from October 17 to 19. During her visit Miss O'Connor was interviewed by three students. The interview was recorded as follows:

**Interviewers:** To whom, or to what do you attribute your view of human nature?

**Miss O'Connor:** Not to anyone. Probably to being a Catholic and a Southerner—and a writer.

**Interviewers:** If the Redemption is a framework for your writing, how do you account for the brutality in your stories?

**Miss O'Connor:** There really isn't much brutality. It always amuses me when people say "brutality." People keep referring to the brutality in the stories, but even "A Good Man Is Hard to Find" is, in a way, a comic, stylized thing. It is not naturalistic writing and so you can't really call it brutal.

**Interviewers:** One critic says that it is grace that leads Bevel to drown himself in the river. Is that true?

**Miss O'Connor:** Bevel hasn't reached the age of reason; therefore he can't commit suicide. He comes to a good end. He's saved from those nutty parents, a fate worse than death. He's been baptized and so he goes to his Maker; this is a good end.

**Interviewers:** Have you ever written a play? Do you plan to eventually write one?

**Miss O'Connor:** That takes a different kind of talent, and I don't have it.

58

**Interviewers:** Why don't Negroes figure more prominently in your stories?

**Miss O'Connor:** I don't understand them the way I do white people. I don't feel capable of entering the mind of a Negro. In my stories they're seen from the outside. The Negro in the South is quite isolated; he has to exist by himself. In the South segregation is segregation.

**Interviewers:** Why are the relationships in *The Violent Bear It Away* all uncle-nephew ones?

**Miss O'Connor:** That's near-enough kin without having to be father-son. Then you get into the son searching for the father sort of thing. Cousins would have been too far apart.

**Interviewers:** Do you think that the writers' course you took at the State University of Iowa helped you learn how to write?

**Miss O'Connor:** Yes, I do. When I went there I didn't know a short story from an ad in a newspaper. I won't say that they taught me how to write, but they gave me that initial push that a writer needs to discover that he can write and that he wants to write.

**Interviewers:** Have you ever considered teaching a writing course?

**Miss O'Connor:** I've always been on the verge, but I've been saved from it.

**Interviewers:** Why are contemporary American writers so little inclined to use classical allusions and references in their writings?

**Miss O'Connor:** Who has a classical education now? I use the Old Testament as my background. But you see, I can because I'm writing about the South. I have a few classical allusions in my stories. There's a reference to Vulcan in "Good Country People."

**Interviewers:** Do you use symbols consciously?

**Miss O'Connor:** Symbols you are conscious of are those that work. All during the story, "Good Country People" the wooden leg is growing in importance. And thus when the Bible salesman steals it, he is stealing a great deal more than the wooden leg. Symbols are big things that knock you in the face.

**Interviewers:** The sun is a common image in your stories. Why?

**Miss O'Connor:** It's there. It's so obvious. And from time immemorial it's been a god.

**Interviewers:** Which story is your favorite?

**Miss O'Connor:** "The Artificial Nigger."

**Interviewers:** What advice would you offer young short story writers.

**Miss O'Connor:** Never go inside a character's head until you know what he looks like. . . . Don't be subtle until the fourth page . . . You have to realize the genuine stupidity of the reader . . . his average mental age is thirteen years.

**Interviewers:** Do you have to write about people you know? Or can you use your imagination?

**Miss O'Connor:** Imagination is a form of knowledge. I don't think you have to know them very well. You discover them.

**Interviewers:** Do you receive many crank letters?

**Miss O'Connor:** Some old lady said that my book left a bad taste in her mouth. I wrote back to her and said, "You weren't supposed to eat it."

# Recent Southern Fiction: A Panel Discussion

Wesleyan College/28 October 1960
Panelists: Katherine Anne Porter, Flannery O'Connor, Caroline
Gordon, Madison Jones, Louis D. Rubin, Jr., Moderator

From *Bulletin of Wesleyan College* [Macon, GA], 41 (January
1961). © 1960 by Wesleyan College. Reprinted by permission.

**Rubin:** I suppose you know what a panel discussion is—for the first
thirty minutes the moderator tries his best to get the panel members
to say something and for the last thirty minutes he does his best to
shut them up. I hope we can do that tonight. My own position here
with these four distinguished Southern writers on my left is
something like the junior member of that famous and often narrated
legal firm—Levy, Ginsberg, Cohen, and Kelly. Kelly presses the suits.
I thought the first thing we might talk about, if we may, would be
writing habits. That is something everyone has one way or another.
Mr. Jones, suppose I ask you, how do you write?

**Jones:** Well, you mean just physically speaking?

**Rubin:** Yes. What time of the day?

**Jones:** Well, I usually write from about 8:30 to 12 or 12:30 in the
morning.

**Gordon:** Every day?

**Jones:** Well, every day except Sunday.

**Gordon:** You're a genius.

**Rubin:** How about you, Miss Porter?

**Porter:** Well, I have no hours at all, just such as I can snatch from
all the other things I do. Once upon a time I tagged a husband
around Europe in the Foreign Service for so many years and never
lived for more than two years in one place and never knew where I
was going to be and I just wrote when I could and I still do. Once in a
while I take the time and run away to an inn and tell them to leave
me alone. When I get hungry, I'll come out. And in those times I
really get some work done. I wrote two short novels in fourteen days

61

once [*Noon Wine* and *Old Mortality*] but that was twenty-five years ago.

**Rubin:** How about you, Miss Gordon?

**Gordon:** I made a horrible discovery this summer. I had a great deal of company and they all wanted to help me with the housework and I discovered I would have to stop writing if I let them do it because my writing and my housework all go together and if they washed the dishes then I didn't get any writing done. That's just my system that I have developed over the years—it works for me except it maddens my friends, because they like to help me wash the dishes.

**Rubin:** You mean your whole day is part of a very closely worked in regimen?

**Gordon:** I didn't discover it until this friend came and insisted she wanted to help me.

**Rubin:** How about you, Miss O'Connor. Do you do your writing along with the dishwashing?

**O'Connor:** Oh, no. I sit there before the typewriter for three hours every day and if anything comes I am there waiting to receive it. I think there should be a complete separation between literature and dishwashing.

**Porter:** I was once washing dishes in an old fashioned dishpan at 11 o'clock at night after a party and all of a sudden I just took my hands up like that and went to the typewriter and wrote the short story "Rope" between that time and two o'clock in the morning. I don't know what started me. I know I had it in mind for several years but the moment came suddenly.

**Rubin:** If that's what dishwashing does, then I'm going to buy a box of Duz in the morning. What I think you all seem to show is that there is no right way or wrong way, I suppose.

**Porter:** I think Grandma Moses is the most charming old soul. When they asked her how she painted—and they meant, I am sure, how she used the brush—she said, "Well, first I saw a masonite board to the size I want the picture to be." And I think that is what we do.

**Rubin:** It all sounds like alchemy to me.

**Gordon:** That is one question that people always ask a writer. How many hours he or she puts in a day. I've often wondered why that is and I just discovered fairly recently. I think they expect you to say you are writing all of the time. If you are mowing the grass you are still thinking about what you are going to write. It is all the time.

**Rubin:** I always remember reading something the late Bernard DeVoto remarked—that one of his hardest jobs was keeping his wife from thinking that if he looked up out of the window, then that meant he wasn't doing any work at the moment, so that she could ask him about some spending money or something of the sort.

**Gordon:** I used to have a dentist—an awfully good one—but I quit him because when he was going to hurt me he would say, "Now just relax and think about your novel." I couldn't take that.

**Jones:** I have always found that when something is going well, I can't think about it at all unless I am right over the paper. Unless I am at work, I can't even get my mind on it away from my environment.

**Rubin:** Let me change the subject. I'll let Miss Porter answer this one. Miss Porter, do you consider yourself a Southern writer?

**Porter:** I am a Southerner. I have been told that I wasn't a Southerner, that anyone born in Texas is a South-westerner. But I can't help it. Some of my people came from Virginia, some from Pennsylvania, but we are all from Tennessee, Georgia, the Carolinas, Kentucky, Louisiana. What does it take to be a Southerner? And being a Southerner, I happen to write so I suppose you combine the two and you have a Southern writer, haven't you? What do you think? I do feel an intense sense of location and of background and my tradition and my country exist to me, but I have never really stuck to it in my writing because I have lived too nomadic a life. You know my people started from Virginia and Pennsylvania toward the West in 1776 or 1777 and none of us really ever stopped since and that includes me. So why should I stick to one place or write about one place since I have never lived just in one place?

**Rubin:** Miss O'Connor, how about you?

**O'Connor:** Well I admit to being one. My own sense of place is quite unadjustable. I have a friend from Michigan who went to Germany and Japan and who wrote stories about Germans who sounded like Germans and about Japanese who sounded like Japanese. I know if I tried to write stories about credible Japanese they would all sound like Herman Talmadge.

**Rubin:** Does the State Department know about *this?* How about you, Mr. Jones?

**Jones:** I feel more or less like Miss O'Connor. No matter where I was or how long I might live there—although my attitude might change—I still have the feeling that everything I would write would be laid in the country that I feel the most communion with, that is the central Tennessee area, or at least a part of it. My imagination just feels at home there. Other places I have been have never tempted me to write about them so I think I am a Southern writer.

**Rubin:** Miss Gordon, how about you?

**Gordon:** I agree with him. I wouldn't think about writing anything about anybody from Princeton. They just don't seem to be important. That's dreadful but that's the way I feel. Your own country—that's the first thing you knew—that's important. I did write one story once that was laid in France but it was fifteen years after I lived there. But I think the thing about the Southern writer—I believe there is such a thing—and I think he is very interesting because he knows something that not all other writers in America today know. I feel that very strongly.

**Porter:** He usually knows who he is and where he is and what he is doing. Some people never know that in a long lifetime. But you see, I write out of my own background about what I know but I can't stay in one place. I write about a country maybe ten years after I have been in it. But that is a part of my experience too, and in a way it is an egotistic thing to do because it is what happened to me. I am writing about my own experience, really, out of my own background and tradition.

**Rubin:** What do you mean by a sense of place? Do you mean simply your geographical knowledge?

**O'Connor:** Not so much the geography. I think it is the idiom. Like Mrs. Tate said, people in Princeton don't talk like we do. And these sounds build up a life of their own in your senses.

**Gordon:** And place is very important too I think.

**Jones:** And I think it is a check in a way, too, of the honesty in your writing. Somehow in writing you have a way to check yourself by the kind of intimacy you have with your community and home.

**Rubin:** I don't think myself there is any doubt that there is such a thing as a Southern Writer—capital S, capital W—and that when you pick up a book, a novel, a short story, it doesn't take you very long before you have the feeling that this is by a Southerner. I suppose

there are Southern writers that fool you. I mean that you don't think
are Southerners. I think that you could pick up some Erskine
Caldwell for instance, particularly his later work, and you would
never think that this man is from 50 miles from where Flannery
O'Connor lives but at the same time—

**Gordon:** But he says things which are not so. For instance, I forget
in what story he has the best hound dogs in the neighborhood down
in the well and all of the men are just sitting around talking. None of
the men are getting the dogs out of the well. That just couldn't
happen. Simply couldn't happen. You can't trust him on detail.

**Rubin:** I like some of the things in the early Caldwell work.

**Gordon:** Oh, at times he's very amusing.

**Rubin:** I was thinking about this the other day. Let's take writers
such as Caldwell and Faulkner or Eudora Welty. You think of them as
being poles apart. But when you compare either of these writers,
with, let's say, Dos Passos, you notice that the Caldwell people and
the Welty people are more or less responsible for their own actions.
In the stuff Caldwell wrote about 1930 or so he was trying to show,
for example, that what was wrong with Jeeter Lester was society and
the share cropping system and things like that, but when he wrote
about Jeeter Lester you couldn't help feeling that the main reason
Jeeter Lester was what he was was because he was Jeeter Lester.
Whereas in a book like *USA* I don't think you had this feeling—I
think you do accept the author's version of experience that society is
what causes it. I think that the individual character somehow being
responsible for his own actions is very typical of the Southern writers,
and I think this is why we have produced very few naturalists as such.
Do you think there is something to that?

**Gordon:** Why I think we have produced wonderful naturalists.

**Rubin:** Well, I was using the word in the literary sense.

**Gordon:** I just don't think you can use it that way. Every good
story has naturalistic elements. Look at the sheep, cows and pigs in
Miss Porter's story, "Holiday."*

**Rubin:** Well, I was using the word in the philosophical sense of the
environment-trapped hero and such as that.

*"Holiday," read by Miss Porter on the preceding evening, appears in the December, 1960 issue of
*The Atlantic.*

**Porter:** Don't you think that came out a great deal in the communist doctrine of the locomotive of history—you know, rounding the sharp bend and everybody who doesn't go with it falls off of it—that history makes men instead of men making history, and it takes away the moral responsibility. The same thing can be said of that cry during the war that nobody could be blamed because we are all guilty until we stopped realizing that one has been guiltier perhaps than the other. This whole effort for the past one hundred years has been to remove the moral responsibility from the individual and make him blame his own human wickedness on his society, but he helps to make his society, you see, and he will not take his responsibility for his part in it.

**Rubin:** Well that's very interesting. I think right there is the difference between Caldwell and Dos Passos. Caldwell was consciously writing out of just that propagandistic position. He wanted to show that these people were victims. Yet because he was a Southerner, because he was writing about these people, they wouldn't behave. They became people instead of symbols.

**Gordon:** I would like to say one other thing about the Southern writer. I think we have some awfully good Southern writers and I believe one reason they are so good is that we are a conquered people and we know some things that a person who is not a Southern writer cannot envisage as happening. For him they never have happened. We know something he does not know.

**Rubin:** You know that this isn't necessarily the greatest nation that ever was or ever will be.

**Gordon:** Well, we know that a nation can go down in defeat. A great many men committed suicide after the Civil War and anyone I have ever heard of left the same note. He said, "This is a great deal worse than I thought it was going to be." Some of them eighty years old. Edmund Ruffin, for example.

**Rubin:** Tell me this now. Do you think that this is as true of the young Southerner growing up today as it was for the generations of Southerners who wrote the books in the 1920's and 30's?

**Gordon:** I think the most terrible thing I have ever read about the South was written by my young friend here [Miss O'Connor]—worse than anything Faulkner ever wrote. That scene where that lady, I forgot her name, but her husband is dead and now she gets in a tight place and she goes into the back hall behind some portieres. I can just see them, too. Some of my aunts had portieres. And she sits down at a roll-top desk which is very dusty and has yellow pieces of paper and things, and communes with his spirit. And his spirit says to her, "One man's meat is another man's poison" or something like "The devil you know is better than the devil you don't know." I think that's the most terrible thing that's ever been written about the South. It haunts me.

**Rubin:** Do you really think that this is changing?

**Gordon:** Well, I would say here is a young writer who has this terrible vision and such a vision could only come out of great concern.

**Rubin:** I wondered though. Nowadays I go to my own home town of Charleston, South Carolina, and it still looks the same downtown but you go outside of the city and everything about it looks just like, well I won't say Newark, New Jersey—it's not that bad—but let's say Philadelphia, and I just wondered if the same environment that operated even on Miss O'Connor will still have the emotional impact that it has had on Southern writing, whether the sense of defeat that we were just mentioning is still going to prevail. I think the notion that the South alone of the American sections knew that it is possible to lose a war, that it is possible to do your very best and still lose, is something that has been very true of Southern life, but I wonder whether in the post-Depression prosperity this is still going to be so? I have a feeling that it isn't.

**Gordon:** I do too.

**Porter:** It is happening already. There are some extremely interesting young writers. Walter Clemons—I don't want to speak of Texas writers altogether—there is one named George Garrett and there are several others—William Humphrey, Peter Taylor, among them, and I think they are probably the last ones who are going to feel the way they do. And I think these young people are probably the last because I don't see anyone coming after them at all and even they have changed a great deal because they don't have the tragic feeling about the South that we had, you know.

**Gordon:** One of Peter's best stories and he says it is his best story is "Bad Time." Do you know that story? It's a beaut.

**Porter:** Yes. But I don't see anybody else coming after and these are greatly changed. You think of young Clemons and then think of ones just before and they are changed. More of them are city people; they are writing about town life. And a kind of life that didn't really interest us, even though we were brought up partly in town. It was the country life that formed us.

**Gordon:** Peter is kind of a missing link. But he writes about country people going to town.

**Jones:** I noticed that in the collection of new Southern writings more than half were set in urban areas.

**Rubin:** You mention William Humphery and to me he is symptomatic of this change. That book [*Home From The Hill*] to me started off extremely well and then suddenly nose-dived, and it nose-dived precisely at the point where the protagonist could no longer do the Faulknerian sort of thing, the hunt and things like that, and was just an adolescent in the city, and it seemed to me we just couldn't take the person seriously enough. Humphrey was still trying to write like Faulkner in a sense—the wrong kind of milieu in the wrong kind of place—and to me the book failed, and this is symptomatic.

**Porter:** He is an extremely good short story writer. He preceded that book with a number of very good short stories, I think, but he did want to write a successful book if he possibly could, you know, and he got the idea of what is success mixed up with what would be good sales and so he spoiled his book by trying to make it popular.

**Rubin:** He succeeded in that.

**Porter:** He did and good luck to him. He was my student for years and I thought he was going to turn out better than that, I must say.

**Rubin:** I have a feeling about the Southern writing in the last ten years, and that includes Miss O'Connor by the way—and I certainly don't mean it as as insult, Miss O'Connor. There is a kind of distance to the life you describe, a kind of esthetic distance, as if the people are far away from the writer, and this sometimes produces an extremely fine emotional effect. Take for example the difference in Styron's *Lie Down in Darkness* and Faulkner's *The Sound and The Fury,* where in both cases you have someone walking around in a northern city holding a time piece getting ready to take his or her life. Somehow or other the protagonist in the Faulkner novel is still a Yoknapatawpha County citizen. Somehow the protagonist in the

Styron novel is away from that, she has left it, she couldn't go back to it if she wanted to or anywhere like that, and to me this feeling runs through so much of the most recent Southern writing. The Southern community is moving farther and farther away. You write about it and do it beautifully, but the distance is farther. You can't take it as seriously.

**Jones:** But don't you think in *Lie Down in Darkness* that as long as he is at home, Styron makes you feel closer to the character? I mean, that last business about the girl seems to be pretty bad.

**Rubin:** What I think about that book is that the book takes place in a Southern city, Port Warwick—something like Newport News, but I don't feel that the family in the book are essentially what they are because of the community at all. I think that is what Mr. Styron wanted them to be. He wanted Payton Loftis to suffer because of several generations, etc., but I don't think she does. I think it is purely because of these particular people involved. Their little private things are apart from the community, and I don't get the same sense of community even when they are writing about things in Port Warwick that you would have in a Faulkner novel.

**Porter:** I have a feeling about Styron, you know the way he develops piles of agonies and horrors and that sort of thing, and I think it masks a lack of feeling. I think he has all the vocabulary of feeling and rhythm of feeling and knows he ought to feel but he does not. I can't read him with any patience at all. I want to say, "Take off those whiskers, come out of the bushes and fight fair."

**Rubin:** I find him a very provocative writer myself.

**Porter:** Well, you remember the story about the man and the two people who come to play cards, I think this was in Rome. They are terrible card cheats and everybody gets frightfully drunk and he winds up perfectly senselessly without any clothes on, robbed and beaten, in a horribly filthy hotel and his wife has to come and get him and you say—now let me see, what was it about? What did it mean? It means absolutely nothing. One feels, well, the police just should have put this one in jail until he sobered up. And such a thing is not interesting for the simple reason that the man to whom it happened is of no interest. That is my quarrel with him, and it is a quarrel, too.

**Rubin:** If there is anything to this feeling of distance, I have the feeling that the Southern writer now isn't taking the things that go on in the community with the same kind of importance. He takes it with equal importance, but with a different kind of importance than, let's say, Faulkner did. Take someone like Sutpen in Faulkner, or Colonel Sartoris. What they did seemed to Faulkner to be very logical and important, even though it may be mad, but at the same time he wasn't writing about it in the sense that he thought he was handling a sort of primitive, or something like that.

**Jones:** Well, in that kind of community I guess that when someone jumps in the water you feel the ripple, but now it is hard to feel it.

**Porter:** I think Styron's trouble may be he really is alienated, you know, from that place and he can't get back home himself. Thomas Wolfe said, "You can't go home again," and I said "Nonsense, that it is the only place you can go. You go there all the time."

**Rubin:** He certainly can't write about Southerners in the sense that they are importantly in the South acting on Southern concerns. His last one takes place in Italy.

**Porter:** It's curious. He may be able to do it. He has been living there for years. But I don't know what is happening to him.

**Rubin:** Miss O'Connor, I know this is a question that writers don't think of and only literary critics like myself think of and ask, but do you think that the Southern community you see, that your relationship to it, is different from the way that Eudora Welty or Faulkner looks at the Southern community?

**O'Connor:** Well, I don't know how either Eudora Welty or Faulkner looks at it. I only know how I look at it and I don't feel that I am writing about the community at all. I feel that I am taking things in the community that I can show the whole western world, the whole edition of the present generation of people, of what I can use of the Southern situation.

**Rubin:** I surely agree with that.

**Porter:** You made that pretty clear yesterday. You know that was one of the things you talked about. It was most interesting.*

**O'Connor:** You know, people say that Southern life is not the way you picture it. Well, Lord help us, let's hope not.

**Rubin:** Well, I think that this is one of the tremendous appeals that

*Miss O'Connor's talk was entitled "Some Thoughts on the Grotesque in Southern Fiction."

Southern writing has had—the universality of its creative materials—but to me there has been some relation between this universality and the particularity with which it is done. You couldn't have one without the other. But I think the fact that you are all writing about the South in the sense that this is the way the people talk, etc., somehow does make possible a meaningful, broader reading that people give it.

**Jones:** It does give you something to check yourself against.

**Rubin:** I think that is a very good notion. It is the thorough grounding in actuality.

**O'Connor:** Well, the South is not the Bible Belt for nothing.

**Porter:** Someone said that the resemblance of the real Southerner to the Frenchman was that we have no organized, impersonal abstract murder. That is, a good Southerner doesn't kill anybody he doesn't know.

**Rubin:** I wonder if even that isn't changing. Speaking of the Bible belt, I think that it has more than one relevance to what we are dealing with. I think it also involves this question of language. I think that Southerners do and did read the Bible a great deal and somehow, more in the King James Bible, this rolling feeling for language comes through.

**Gordon:** They read a lot of Cicero, too.

**O'Connor:** More than the language it seems to me it is simply the concrete, the business of being a story teller. I have Boston cousins and when they come South they discuss problems, they don't tell stories. We tell stories.

**Rubin:** Well look now, how about our audience? I am sure that our panel will be glad to parry any questions you would like to throw at them. Doesn't someone have a question or two to ask?

**Question:** Would someone care to comment on the great number of old people and children in Southern writing?

**Porter:** Well, they are very much there.

**Gordon:** How many children in that family you were reading about last night?

**Porter:** Well, there were eight under the age of ten—counting one not yet born—belonging to two women. That isn't bad, is it? And I have known them to do better than that. And with the old people who always seem to live forever and everybody always lived in the same house, all the generations. It was one way of getting acquainted with the generations. We simply would have old people and we would have children in the house together, and they were important, both ends of the line. It was really the ones in mid-life who took the gaff, didn't they? Because they had the young on one side and the old on the other.

**Rubin:** They were too young to be tolerated and not old enough to be characters.

**Porter:** A friend of mine said the other day, "Now there are only three degrees of age—young, mature and remarkable."

**Question:** Miss O'Connor, you said yesterday that the South was Christ-haunted instead of Christ-centered. I don't quite understand this and how it effects our Southern literature. Would you please explain this?

**O'Connor:** I shouldn't have said that, should I? Well, as I said, the South didn't seem to me as a writer to be Christ-centered. I don't think anyone would object to that at all. I think all you would have to do is to read the newspapers to agree with me, but I said that we seemed to me to be Christ-haunted and that ghosts cast strange shadows, very fierce shadows, particularly in our literature. It is hard to explain a flat statement like that. I would hate to talk off the top of my head on a subject like that. I think it is a subject that a book could be written about but it would take me ten or twelve years to do it.

**Gordon:** When I was young, old gentlemen sat under the trees reading. That was all they did all of the time, and shall we call it the movement which is sometimes called The Death of God, that controversy that Hegel the Philosopher had with Heine the Poet. There was quite a lot of talk about the death of God, but God crossed the border, and I think that is what you are talking about. It's cast its shadow.

**O'Connor:** It's gone underneath and come out in distorted forms.

**Question:** I would like particularly Miss Porter to comment on religious symbolism in her work—if you think there is any and how you go about it in your work.

**Porter:** Symbolism happens of its own self and it comes out of something so deep in your own consciousness and your own experience that I don't think that most writers are at all conscious of their use of symbols. I never am until I see them. They come of themselves because they belong to me and have meaning to me, but they come of themselves. I have no way of explaining them but I have a great deal of religious symbolism in my stories because I have a very deep sense of religion and also I have a religious training. And I suppose you don't invent symbolism. You don't say, "I am going to have the flowering Judas tree stand for betrayal," but, of course, it does.

**O'Connor:** I would second everything Miss Porter says. I really didn't know what a symbol was until I started reading about them. It seemed I was going to have to know about them if I was going to be a respectable literary person. Now I have the notion that a symbol is sort of like the engine in a story and I usually discover as I write something in the story that is taking on more and more meaning so that as I go along, before long, that something is turning or working the story.

**Rubin:** Do you ever have to try to stop yourselves from thinking about your work in terms of symbols as you are working?

**O'Connor:** I wouldn't say so.

**Porter:** No, May I tell this very famous little story about Mary McCarthy and symbols. Well, she was in a college and she had a writers' class and there was a young person who wrote her a story and she said, "You have done a very nice piece of work. You are on the right road, now go on to something else." And the young person said, "But my teacher read this and said, 'Well all right, but now we have to go back and put in the symbols.'"

**Rubin:** How about you, Mr. Jones?

**Jones:** Am I a symbol man? Well, I don't think so. The story is the thing after all and I don't see how a writer can think about anything but the story. The story has got to carry him. I think it is bound to occur to you finally that something you have come across—maybe in the middle of coming across it it might occur to you—that this has certain symbolic value and maybe you would to a certain extent elaborate it in terms of this realization, but I don't think it is a plan of any kind where you say I am heading for a symbol and when I get there I am going to do so and so to it. It just comes out of the context. Of course, writing is full of symbols. Nearly everything is a symbol of some kind but some of them expand for you accidentally.

**O'Connor:** So many students approach a story as if it were a problem in algebra: find X and when they find X they can dismiss the rest of it.

**Porter:** Well and then another thing, everything can be used as a symbol. Take two of the most innocent and charming sounding, for example, just in western Christianity, let us say the dove and the rose. Well, the dove begins by being a symbol of sensuality, it is the bird of Venus, you know, and then it goes on through the whole range of every kind of thing until it becomes the Holy Ghost. It's the same way with the rose which begins as a female sexual symbol and ends as the rose of fire in Highest Heaven. So you see the symbol would have the meaning of its context. I hope that makes sense.

**Question:** Is tradition an important part of contemporary Southern writing?

**Rubin:** What about you, Miss Gordon, do you have a tradition you go back to when you are writing? You told me today that you are writing an historical novel.

**Gordon:** All novels are historical. I don't think I told you I was writing an historical novel. I said it went back to 1532.

**Rubin:** Well, that sounds pretty historical.

**Gordon:** The word has become so debased. I wrote two novels, one in Civil War times and one in pioneer times, but people didn't know how to read them. I wouldn't like to be accused of writing what is known as an historical novel.

**Rubin:** Well, instead of saying tradition, do you think Southerners do things in certain ways because that is the way they have always been done rather than thinking about it at all, and if so, is this the way you see the Southerner in what you write?

**Gordon:** Well, I don't see it that way. I sit there or I walk around or I wash dishes until I see these people doing something and hear them and then I record it as best I can.

**Rubin:** It is very hard to get people to talk in terms of these abstractions because I don't think anyone uses tradition with a capital T. And yet there is a lot of tradition in what they do.

**Question:** I meant white columns, magnolias, worship of family— tradition in this sense.

**Gordon:** Well, after the Civil War there was a school of literature foisted on us by Northern publishers. They demanded moonlight and magnolias and a lot of people furnished it to them and that idea stuck in peoples' heads ever since. If a Southerner writes a novel now, whoever is reviewing for the *New York Times* will make a point of saying it isn't moonlight and magnolias. It's all nonsense. We are a conquered nation and abominably treated and we paid the greatest tribute perhaps ever paid by any conquered nation. Our history was miswritten and our children were taught lies and therefore the Northerners could not bear the image of us as we were and therefore the Northern publishers would publish only novels full of white columns and magnolias.

**Porter:** But this very place right this minute is absolutely filled to the chin with moonlight and magnolias. All you have to do is look outside.

**Rubin:** I think the position of that particular role of moonlight and magnolias tradition in Southern literature is very true. In the case of someone like George Washington Cable, for example. He tried to write one book without it and it was a flop. Nobody paid any attention to it so he went back and wrote the flowery sort of war romances. This was the only thing he could write. I must say that this ain't so no more, and I think it has been people like Miss Porter who ended all that. Many people read their books for what the books *say*, instead of what the people *thought* they should say. I think that the tremendous importance of Southern literature in our own time represents a breaking away from the stereotype. Writers who have done this, having published their first books in the 20's and 30's, have performed a great service for future generations of Southern writers. Not that that was what you were trying to do at the time, but I think the young ones are going to be eternally grateful for it.

**O'Connor:** Walker Percy wrote somewhere that his generation of Southerners had no more interest in the Civil War than in the Boer War. I think that is probably quite true.

**Rubin:** I think there is something to that and yet I heard many an argument in the Army during the last war. You get one or two Southerners in a barracks with a bunch of Northerners and maybe the Southerners were just kidding but let anyone say anything too outrageous and the fight was on.

**Jones:** That's true. They'll still fight but they don't know what they are talking about. They have no real information and so it is more a matter of just being a personal insult.

**Question:** Do you think that the South is being exploited now for its immediate fictional gains, let's say commercial gain, etc., is it too popular? Is it too much *Southern* writing?

**O'Connor:** I don't know any Southern writers who are making a big killing except Faulkner, you know. We are all just limping along.

**Rubin:** I think when you have a group of very fine writers who approach a group of people and subjects in a certain way it is then easier to imitate that than to do something on your own. And therefore a lot of second rate writers will come along and imitate it, and I know I see the publisher announcement sheets every fall. On one page of almost all announcement sheets from every publishing house there is announced a new Southern writer and most of them are never announced more than once. But I do feel very definitely there is a great deal of writing about the South, because these people here have shown how it can be done, and therefore someone is not going to do something on his or her own when this is the best lead to follow.

**Question:** I would like to know if your writing is strictly for a Southern reading audience or if you have in mind any reading audience.

**O'Connor:** The *London Times Literary Supplement* had an issue on Southern writing once and they said that Southerners only wrote books, they didn't read them.

**Porter:** Well, that's just the opposite from the old South because they only read them, they never wrote them. At least before The War Between the States writing was not really a gentleman's occupation except as privately. He wrote letters, memoirs, and maybe essays. But they all had libraries and collections of books.

**Rubin:** The South has long had the reputation for being the worst market for books in the U.S., per capita, among the publishers. I think any Southern writer who wrote primarily for Southerners would have to write a syndicated column for a newspaper or he would starve to death. I don't really think that these people think in terms of who is going to read what they are going to write, unless I am mistaken.

**Jones:** I was just going to say that I don't know who I write for but it seems to me that I have a person or two who is my audience rather than any group. But I think about one person and perhaps the standards that I absorbed from that person tends to be my audience rather than any group. I hope that a group will buy a book but I don't think I direct a book at any large group of people.

**Rubin:** John Bishop wrote that he wrote his books to be read by Edmund Wilson and Allen Tate.

**Gordon:** But you see he never wrote but one novel. Well, I know I have one reader, a Frenchman. He is the only person I know of who understands my work and I think that is why I think about him but I don't think I would under other circumstances. He knows a great deal about techniques of fiction and, perhaps this is a little off the subject, but people very much dislike any revolution in technique. If an author uses a technique that has never been used before, everybody will dislike it. And there is no record of any literary critic ever recognizing an innovation in technique. It has never happened. It is always recognized by another artist. So I have gotten to the point that I write for the person who will know what I am doing.

**Question:** Mr. Jones, you mentioned this afternoon that Southern writers have a stronger than usual sense of guilt and natural depravity. If this is so, what means of redemption do you see as possible?

**Jones:** You asked me a very complex question. I don't know whether I can answer the whole thing or not. You said that Southern writers have a sense of natural depravity. Do I think they do? Well, I do have the feeling that if it is not still, it certainly was the case with the first important Southern writers in that there was very little question about the sense of man's guilt. There was a consciousnesss of that and a perfect willingness to accept it and I think that is very notable in all the best Southern writers of the last generation. I don't know why that should particularly be the case with Southern writers except partly because, as I said, of Southern Fundamentalism which has kept that fact before them. And perhaps the Civil War had something to do with it. Not that I feel that the Southerners felt guilty about the Civil War but perhaps even though we felt we were right before the war, nevertheless we were defeated and didn't achieve all we thought we could even though we thought we were right and something must be wrong. I am sure there would be a great many other reasons that someone else could elaborate on. Man is of a less than perfect nature.

**Porter:** I am sure that we are all naturally depraved but we are all naturally redeemable, too. The idea, Calvin really put it into action, that God somehow rewarded spiritual virtue with material things, which is to say that if you were living right God would reward you with health and money, a good reputation, or the goods of this world is to me an appalling doctrine. I happen to have a faith that says the opposite, you see, that goods of this world have nothing to do with your spiritual good and your standing with God and I think that this attitude of the South, when you say they felt that if they had been right God would not have permitted them to lose that war is dreadful, you know. I think it is a terrible fallacy and a terrible mistaken way to feel because some very good people have had the worst times in this world and have lost all their wars, don't you know, have lost everything altogether. Defeat in this world is no disgrace and that is what they cannot understand. If you really fought well and fought for the right thing.

**Rubin:** That is a very good point. You know, I think it is about time we finished. I would like to question you a bit on that Calvin business if it weren't. I think we had better say one thing. We have been talking about a number of characteristics and we say, now *this* is Southern, and *this* Southern, and then somebody comes along and says, well don't you think that New England writers, or Western writers, have a notion about the natural depravity of man? Is this something that was invented in the South? I think the answer would be is that there are a number of qualities that people assign to Southern writing and say, "This is true of Southern writing." It isn't the uniqueness of the qualities, but I would say the combination of a certain number of qualities at one time, which has made this achievement possible and I think that whatever the achievement is, it has been a considerable thing; and I, myself, am not particularly pessimistic about it continuing, what with the people seated at the table with me tonight. We have hashed over the problems of writers and writing in the South for about an hour now and tried to answer some questions, and I think we'll quit. I would like to say on behalf of the panel what a wonderful time we have had and how grateful we are to Wesleyan College and to everybody for coming.

# Authoress Flannery O'Connor is Evidence of Georgia's Bent to the Female Writer

Betsy Fancher/April 1961

From *The Atlanta Constitution,* 21 April 1961, 27. © 1961 by The Atlanta Constitution. Reprinted by permission.

Is it merely coincidence that Georgia's four major writers are women?

After 25 years *Gone With the Wind*, by the late Margaret Mitchell, is still a year in, year out best seller. Two novellas, *Member of the Wedding* and *Ballad of the Sad Cafe,* by Carson McCullers, a native of Columbus, have become classics.

Critics now are awaiting a forthcoming biography of Lafcadio Hearn by Atlanta's Elizabeth Stevenson, a Bancroft award winner.

And Milledgeville's Flannery O'Connor, a three-time winner of the O. Henry Short-story award, is the author of one of 1960's most widely acclaimed novels. *The Violent Bear It Away.*

But Miss O'Connor, visiting the Agnes Scott College campus this week for the Fine Arts Festival now in progress, sees no particular reason for the feminine hold on Georgia letters.

"Women just have more time," she says matter-of-factly.

Although she lives on a farm, amid rolling green acres outside of Milledgeville, she devotes all her time to serious fiction. "I hardly ever look out of the window," she says of her environment.

With the exception of Miss Stevenson, whose subjects have been Henry Adams, Henry James and Lafcadio Hearn, Georgia's women writers have taken their themes from the paradoxes, the tragedies and conflicts of this region.

Will the growing industrialization and sweeping social changes taking place here change the tenor of Southern literature?

Inevitably, says Miss O'Connor. "But there's not too much evidence of it yet."

And yet she also believes that "the writer has no responsibility to topical subjects."

His province is the "human condition which he may approach indirectly through individuals, be they black or white.

He need not be politically concerned," she said this week.

The young (thirtyish), brown-haired, winsome writer is concerned this week with the work of Agnes Scott students. The beginning writer in college "is just learning his limitations," she points out.

But she praised the work of Scott students, published in the campus magazine *Aurora*, found it "superior to most I have seen."

# A Writer at Home
# with Her Heritage
Granville Hicks/April 1962

From *Saturday Review*, 45 (12 May 1962), 22-23. © 1962
Saturday Review Magazine. Reprinted by permission.

MILLEDGEVILLE, capital of the state from 1807 to 1868, seems to the
Northern visitor exactly what a Southern town ought to be. If it is less
picturesque than Charleston, it is perhaps even more impressive, for
here one finds one mansion after another, each with its white
columns, each with its lawns and its gardens, full just now of azalea
and dogwood, though both are passing. Located in the center of
town is the campus of the Woman's College of Georgia, whose
president occupies what was once the Governor's mansion.

Milledgeville people are proud of their town, and with reason.
Many are also proud that this is the home of Flannery O'Connor,
whom they know as a person and admire as a novelist and writer of
short stories. ("Which do you like better," they ask at teas, "her
novels or her short stories?")

Miss O'Connor lives with her mother on the outskirts of town in a
farmhouse built early in the nineteenth century. It is not a mansion
but a real farmhouse, a substantial, unpretentious, two-story building.
This is a plantation of some 500 acres, devoted to the raising of beef
cattle, and there are horses in the fields and a variety of domestic
fowl about the house. But one is most aware of the peafowl, which
are Miss O'Connor's particular enthusiasm. She doesn't know, she
says, just how many of them there are—twenty-five or thirty. They
are everywhere one looks, the cocks strutting about the yard, and
crying out at us from shed roofs, and periodically, for this is the right
season, spreading their incredible tails.

Miss O'Connor is on crutches, which she has had to use for the
past six years as a result of disseminated lupus. "They don't interfere

with anything," she says, and they don't seem to. She is a pleasant, poised, quiet young woman, rather inscrutable—or perhaps I think that only because I have read her work—but instantly likable. She talks well, answering questions concisely and without the least hesitation, and I have no doubt that she is a woman who knows her mind.

We begin with Milledgeville. She has spent a good part of her life here, but not all. She was born in Savannah, but she moved to Milledgeville, which had been the home of her mother's family for several generations, when she was a girl, and she attended college here. Afterwards she studied for three years at the University of Iowa, devoting most of her time to writing. She spent a winter at Yaddo, several months in New York City, and two years in Connecticut. But for ten years she has been living on this farm, and, she says, it is exactly where she wants to live.

She is not at all, as some reporters have suggested, a recluse. Fairly often she goes away to lecture or to read her work. (She had just returned from North Carolina State College when I saw her, was leaving in a few days for a conference at Converse, had a later engagement at Notre Dame.) She has many friends in Milledgeville whom she visits and is visited by. She corresponds with writers in various parts of the country, and sometimes they come to see her. All in all, she thinks she has quite enough contact with the literary life: "I think you can see too much of writers; I don't like writers' talk."

She is definite about her working schedule: "I write from nine to twelve, and spend the rest of the day recuperating from it." She reads, she tells me, watches the peacocks, and talks to people. She used to paint a little, but the crutches make the preparation for painting a tedious job. (As a matter of fact, her friends once expected her to be a painter rather than a writer.)

She has no doubt that, as a writer, she belongs in Georgia. Some Southern writers, she acknowledges, can be successfully cosmopolitan, and she cites Katherine Anne Porter; but she is sure that she herself could not. ("If I went to Japan and tried to write credible stories about Japanese, all my Japanese would sound like Herman Talmadge.") Her ear is tuned to Georgia speech and since she regards the ear as one of the writer's major assets, she does not want to lose any of her sensitivity.

Recently, in praising Marion Montgomery's *The Wandering of Desire,* Miss O'Connor said that any Southern writer has two great advantages—a knowledge of the Bible and a sense of history. Certainly here in Milledgeville the visitor, even a visitor with roots in New England, is impressed by the feeling people have for the continuity of experience. As for the Bible, Miss O'Connor asserts that it is still a great power in the South and that it continues to influence the Southern writer. For one thing, it conditions him to think in concrete terms: "We don't discuss problems; we tell stories." More important, the Bible gives meaning and dignity to the lives of the poor people of the South, and the writer, particularly the Christian writer, has something in common with them.

Her comments on this point naturally lead me to ask Miss O'Connor why she, a Catholic, has written about Fundamentalist Protestants in both of her novels, *Wise Blood* and *The Violent Bear It Away,* and many short stories. Her answer is quiet but emphatic. "I'm not interested in the sects as sects; I'm concerned with the religious individual, the backwoods prophet. Old Tarwater is the hero of *The Violent Bear It Away,* and I'm right behind him 100 per cent."

Since there are not many Catholics in Miss O'Connor's part of Georgia, she has to write about Protestants, and she finds such characters as Old Tarwater completely congenial. He is, she suggests, a crypto-Catholic: "He lacks the visible Church, but Christ is the center of his life." His religion is closer to hers than either the outright secularism or the diluted Protestantism of the North. Being a Catholic in the South, she thinks, may help a novelist to understand both the South and Catholicism more clearly.

I ask her about her relationship with Milledgeville: doesn't she feel alienated both as a writer and as a Catholic? She doesn't think so. People accept her as a person, and that is all that matters: "If I cared what they thought about what I write, I'd have dried up a long time ago." As a Catholic, of course, she is a member of a minority group, but it is a group that has long been recognized by the community. The first mass said in Milledgeville was said in her great-grandfather's hotel room, and another ancestor gave the ground on which the local Catholic church stands. It would be ridiculous, she feels, to suggest that she is alienated from Milledgeville because she is a Catholic.

In short, she has no complaints about her situation as a writer.

What she has here is what she wants and what she can use. At North Carolina State College, she tells me, she spoke on "The Grotesque in Southern Fiction." Her argument, I gather, was that in these times the most reliable path to reality, to the kind of reality that seems to her important, is by way of the grotesque. The grotesque, she puts it, is more real than the real, and what many people regard as the real seems to her more grotesque than any of the characters she has created. Her vision of life is given her by Catholicism; the material with which she works is provided by the South. Natural endowment and firm discipline have done the rest.

# Off the Cuff
Joel Wells/May 1962

From *The Critic*, 21 (August-September 1962), 4-5, 71-72. ©
1962 *The Critic*. Reprinted by permission.

Early this May, one of my favorite writers of fiction, Flannery
O'Connor, came north from her home near Milledgeville, Georgia,
for a three-day stay at Rosary College in Chicago's suburb of River
Forest. In spite of being on crutches (for the past six years due to an
affliction called disseminated lupus) she travels frequently and alone.
She had already been to a conference at Converse and to North
Carolina State University before taking up the invitation to Rosary
where she presided at five classes, gave an hour's talk to the entire
student body and was the featured attraction at a tea.

Though understandably a little done in, she agreed to talk to me
while I drove her from Rosary to South Bend, where she was due to
speak at Notre Dame on "The Catholic Writer in the Protestant
South." I met her at one o'clock on an unseasonably warm day and,
after making our farewells to a Rosary delegation obviously sorry to
yield her up, we got underway. Speaking in a soft and, to Chicago-
hardened ears, definitely drawling voice, she said that the Rosary
students had amazed her with their close knowledge of her work,
sometimes to the point of embarrassing her by citing things which
roosted on the very edge of her own memory. Her only complaint
was the temperature of the buildings, which stuck her as having
hovered just above freezing most of the time. She admitted that this
was probably psychological on her part since she had once come to
Chicago in the dead cold of winter and had never fully recovered
from the experience. About her forthcoming talk at Notre Dame she
expressed doubts as to having much of a crowd since she understood
she was going on in direct and simultaneous competition with the
Junior Prom.

I asked her if she had any qualms about driving with an unknown quantity of roadsmanship such as I must surely represent to her. She said with candor (Miss O'Connor is a candid person: to a question as to what she thought of Tennessee Williams she replied, "Not much;" and her opinion of *To Kill a Mockingbird* is that "it's a wonderful children's book") that she was willing to risk almost anything as opposed to lurching about on a train with her crutches or the strong possibility of having to fly the ninety miles to South Bend in a "small plane," a species of aircraft which she identified with more emotion than precision as any that had to be boarded "near the tail on rickety tin steps." In the same spirit, I told her that I had illogical but real misgivings about driving with her since so many terrible things seem always to happen to people in her stories while they are out driving. She assured me that such things happen only in the South.

In the middle lane of Chicago's teeming Congress Street Expressway, flanked and bracketed by enormous and odiferous deisel trucks, Miss O'Connor may well have upgraded sharply her opinion of small planes, but she showed no visible signs of distress. Since I was not going to be able to hear her talk at Notre Dame (for which, as it turned out, a good crowd of non-dancers did appear), I asked her whether she felt that being a Catholic writer in the South made her task as a novelist more difficult.

Some Northerners, for instance, seem to have a hard time believing that characters such as those with which she peoples her stories could possibly exist—the whole burden of their creation must rest on her talents without any helpful assistance from real-life prototypes. Then there is the additional obstacle that Northerners in general, and Catholics in particular, don't seem to look at life and religion in the biblical light that colors so much of Southern fiction. Did this leave her in a predicament—somewhat documented by sales figures—of facing heavy odds against wide popular understanding?

This was quite a woolly question, but Miss O'Connor who is not only candid but graciously tolerant, took it at more than face value. The people she writes about, she said, are real. Not in the literal sense of being copies from life, but as types which still exist in the South, not evident to tourists perhaps, but there all the same. They are real, and if they are people who deal with life on more

fundamental, even more violent terms than most of us, this doesn't
make them mythical monsters.

As for the lack of biblical understanding, she said: "The fact that
Catholics don't see religion through the Bible is a deficiency in
Catholics. And I don't think the novelist can discard the instruments
he has to plumb meaning just because Catholics aren't used to them.
You don't write only for now. The biblical revival is going to mean a
great deal to Catholic fiction in the future. Maybe in fifty years, or a
hundred, Catholics will be reading the Bible the way they should
have been reading it all along. I can wait that long to have my fiction
understood. The Bible is what we share with all Christians, and the
Old Testament we share with all Jews. This is sacred history and our
mythic background. If we are going to discard this we had better quit
writing at all. The fact that the South is the Bible Belt is in great
measure responsible for its literary preeminence now. The Catholic
novelist can learn a great deal from the Protestant South."

I cited one of her college talks in which she had said "for the
modern reader, moral distinctions are usually blurred in hazes of
compassion; there are not enough common beliefs to make this a fit
age for allegory; and as for anagogical realities, they either don't exist
at all for the general reader or are taken by him to be knowable by
sensation." Did she think that this was the basic problem confronting
the Christian novelist? Could this eventually be so limiting that such a
writer will have to be content with writing only for a few.

"One of the Christian novelist's basic problems is that he is trying
to get the Christian vision across to an audience to whom it is
meaningless," Miss O'Connor agreed. "Nevertheless, he can't write
only for a select few. His work will have to have value on the
dramatic level, the level of truth recognizable by anybody. The fact
that many people can't see anything Christian about my novel
doesn't interfere with many of them seeing it as a novel which does
not falsify reality."

I wondered if she was generally pleased with the critical reception
given her most recent novel—*The Violent Bear It Away*—not in a
vain sense, but simply with regard to the measure of understanding
she saw evidenced. I mentioned Orville Prescott's review for the
New York *Times* in which he had said that while her talent for fiction

was "so great as to be almost overwhelming," he had been unable to see any evidence of the Christian relationships she intended to convey, according to her own intentions set down in an article he had read in a symposium called *The Living Novel,* edited by Granville Hicks.

Miss O'Connor felt that this was a good example of what we had just been talking about. "If Mr. Prescott hadn't read that article I wrote for Granville Hicks he wouldn't have been looking so hard for relationships and would have taken it just as a novel," she said. "There were enough Catholic reviews which shared my own interpretation of it for me to feel that I succeeded well enough in doing what I intended to do." She mentioned one review in particular which appeared in the 1962 issue of an annual called *Kansas Magazine.* "It was written by a Jesuit Scholastic, Robert McCown, whom I had never met or corresponded with beforehand. But he seemed to understand everything I did about the book."

What about those reviews which seemed to imply that she had tried to fit too great a burden of meaning to her novel, been too allegorical, too much and too obviously the careful builder? There were a few who came close to saying that she had tried too hard— that in her short stories she was the pure artist at work but in her novels, a great artist still, but one more obviously on the moral make. Had she consciously set out to get a bigger message across in the novels?

"Message," said Miss O'Conner, still being candid, "is a bad word. It took me seven years to write *The Violent Bear It Away* and I hope there's more to it than a short story. As for its being too allegorical and all the rest, I can't agree. I wanted to get across the fact that the great Uncle (Old Tarwater) is the Christian—a sort of crypto-Catholic—and that the school teacher (Rayber) is the typical modern man. The boy (young Tarwater) has to choose which one, which way, he wants to follow. It's a matter of vocation."

I asked if she would amplify something she had said to the effect that there are ages when it is possible to woo the reader and others when something more drastic is necessary. Did she deliberately set out to be more drastic in her work?

"I don't consciously set out to be more drastic," she said, "but this happens automatically. If I write a novel in which the central action is a baptism, I know that for the larger percentage of my readers, baptism is a meaningless rite; therefore I have to imbue this action with an awe and terror which will suggest its awful mystery. I have to distort the look of the thing in order to represent as I see them both the mystery and the fact."

Since there is (to my mind) a great deal of very rich humor in almost everything Miss O'Connor has written (among her stories she names as favorite a wryly comic little masterpiece called "The Artificial Nigger"), and also an evident and deep concern with religious and prophetic values, I was interested in getting her reaction to something that Evelyn Waugh had once said. In an interview recorded in Harvey Breit's *The Writer Observed,* Mr. Waugh talked about people—Protestants in particular—who thought that a religious subject could never be treated with humor. He felt that most young contemporary writers had lost all their delight in the material, that they wrote believing they had some sort of message to deliver from their souls. He stated his own belief that words should be an intense pleasure in themselves, just as leather is to a shoemaker. People who didn't take that pleasure from writing, Mr. Waugh suggested, should become philosophers instead. And in any case, writers had no right to be like Lawrence or Hemingway, thinking they were prophets.

"I agree with Mr. Waugh that words should be an intense pleasure," said Miss O'Connor, "but I don't see the connection between this and his rejection of a prophetic function for the writer. It seems to me that prophetic insight is a quality of the imagination and that Waugh is as prophetic in this sense as the next one. There is the prophetic sense of 'seeing through' reality and there is also the prophetic function of recalling people to known but ignored truths. Certainly none of this precludes comedy—or the pleasure taken in producing it."

I had already heard from Sister Mary Bryan, Miss O'Connor's sponsor at Rosary College, that she had responded to questions as to what she intended to do when she got home by saying, "An awful lot of porch-settin'." She has no new novel underway, much as she wished she had. A long short story, amounting almost to a novella, was the most recent thing she had done and it would appear in the Summer issue of *The Sewanee Review.* She feels that her short stories don't seem to get any better but she intends to keep on writing them until another novel takes shape in her mind. She thinks it takes time to write good fiction, and knows it takes her a long time. Besides the two novels (her first was *Wise Blood* which will be brought out in a new edition this fall by Farrar, Straus & Cudahy) she has produced a total of seventeen short stories, not counting a few she chooses to forget.

I wondered if she had ever considered writing a play, or letting someone adapt any of her work for the stage or movies. She didn't think she would ever write a play herself, mainly because she wouldn't know how to go about it. One man has repeatedly expressed interest in producing a movie of her story "The River" but seems just as repeatedly hamstrung by lack of money. The Schlitz Playhouse presented a television adaption of another story, "The Life You Save May Be Your Own," in which an itinerant no-good agreed to marry a widow's idiot daughter to gain title to her car. He does, but after driving a hundred miles or so, abandons the girl in a roadside diner.

"I didn't recognize the television version," said Miss O'Connor, "Gene Kelly played Mr. Shiftlet and for the idiot daughter they got some young actress who had just been voted one of the ten most beautiful women in the world, and they changed the ending just a bit by having Shiftlet suddenly get a conscience and come back for the girl."

It was at this point that we reached the toll road exit for South Bend and turned off to drive along the road which separates the Notre Dame campus from St. Mary's College, where Miss O'Connor would be returning at commencement time to receive an honorary Doctor of Letters degree.

All in all, she admitted, thanking me for the ride, traveling with me had turned out to be better than in a small plane—though she probably wouldn't have had to talk so much on the plane.

As Truman Capote said of her, "She has some fine moments, that girl!"

# Flannery O'Connor Shapes Own Capital
Frank Daniel/21 July 1962

From *The Atlanta Journal and The Atlanta Constitution,* 22 July
1962, sec. C, 2. © 1962 The Atlanta Journal and The Atlanta
Constitution. Reprinted by permission.

"Free will does not mean one will, but many wills conflicting," said
Flannery O'Connor. She spoke in the living room of her pleasant
home near Georgia's Civil War capital.

And single-handedly she has made her community another
capital—a literary one, for the novels and stories she writes slowly,
diligently, prayerfully have established her with the finest younger
writers today.

More and more she must interrupt her daily writing to deal with
visitors who seek an understanding of her extraordinary talent and
insight.

Their visits do not much distract her. She seems to accept
interviewers as philosophically as she has accepted the illness from
which she is recovering, but which may keep her dependent on
crutches for uncomfortable years.

Meanwhile, she is finding outlets for her mental and physical
energies in her work and in her surroundings. The authority with
which she wrote *The Violent Bear It Away* leaves the reader with an
impression of sureness, self-confidence.

"I write every day. But often nothing comes of my efforts. They
don't lead anywhere. I rewrite, edit, throw away. It's slow and
searching. I'm not sure until it is down on paper."

For a travel magazine she has written a story, not about traveling,
but about the unfashionable idea of staying at home. She
recommends that course of action. And she told about her peafowls,
and the burros, and the various activities and interests she and her
mother enjoy on their 500-acre farm—which they call Andalusia,

revealing in the harmonious word that they have, at least, let their fancies roam.

Paintings by Miss O'Connor hang in several rooms of her home. Asked if painting is a relaxation, she said it isn't—that it is hard work.

"Maybe more so because I know nothing about it. I painted these pictures when we moved into the house, because the walls needed pictures. When I'd filled up the space, I stopped until we added on a couple of rooms a couple of years ago. The new sitting room needed a picture in a wall space, so I painted one. That done, I've painted no more."

Just now Miss O'Connor is interested in her swans. She had always wanted them. But swans are expensive. So she compromised on peafowl, of which she has about 30. But she compromised only temporarily. When she heard a Florida swanfarm was going out of business she communicated with the owners. They offered her swans at $250 each. Too much.

There was, however, one pair for sale at less, because one of the pair had only one eye. Miss Flannery took them. They are on her farm, and she is anxiously waiting for them to nest.

"I was told they were mates, but so far they haven't given much evidence of it. You know swans mate for life. But I'm hopeful. Maybe it's the change of scene."

The male swan is a cob. What is the female called? Miss O'Connor supplied the information: "A pen."

"Pen?" you ask, "or hen?"

"Pen," Miss O'Connor insists. Why? She didn't know. Possibly short for Penelope, who remained faithful to Odysseus for 20 years — which some folks might feel is running even constancy into the ground.

In evidence of Miss O'Connor's literary prestige, her first book, *Wise Blood,* is being reissued. Invited to edit it, bring it up to date, Miss O'Connor was content with this brief introduction.

"*Wise Blood* has reached the age of 10 and is still alive. My critical powers are just sufficient to determine this, and I am gratified to be able to say it. The book was written with zest and, if possible, it should be read that way.

"It is a comic novel about a Christian *malgré lui*, and as such, very serious, for all comic novels that are any good must be about matters of life and death.

"*Wise Blood* was written by an author congenitally innocent of theory, but one with certain preoccupations. That belief in Christ is to some a matter of life and death has been a stumbling block for readers who prefer to think it is a matter of no great consequence.

"For them Hazel Motes' integrity (Hazel Motes is the hero of *Wise Blood*) lies in his trying with such vigor to get rid of the ragged figure who moves from tree to tree in the back of his mind. For the author, Hazel's integrity lies in his not being able to.

"Does one's integrity ever lie in what he is not able to do? I think that usually it does, for free will will does not mean one will, but many wills conflicting in man. Freedom cannot be conceived simply. It is a mystery and one which a novel, even a comic novel, can only be asked to deepen."

Why did Miss O'Connor call her hero "Hazel"? Because she has observed that rural families often give their sons names usually considered feminine names—June, for instance.

*Wise Blood* in its new format will be published again on Aug. 31. It first appeared in 1952, and is concerned with a man of humble, rural background, who believes he may be called to preach.

*The Violent Bear It Away* has a similar theme, more boldly and expertly developed, perhaps more moving in its clarity and glow. It appeared in 1960, after five years in the writing. Miss O'Connor's short stories, *A Good Man Is Hard to Find,* were published in book form in 1955.

All these have been published in England. The volume of short stories contains one titled "The Artificial Nigguh," and the English publisher gave that name to the volume. It has led to Miss O'Connor dissolving her contract with this publisher. She feels the change might have been made for sensationalism.

The title has given her considerable trouble. When the story first appeared, it was accepted on condition that the title be changed.

Clearly Miss O'Connor felt that implication was necessary in the story she told. The phrase comes about when a stranger in a rural Georgia community asks to be directed to a certain house. A native tells the inquirer he can't miss it.

"It's the only house around that's got an artificial nigguh," the informant says. He is referring to one of those plaster-of-Paris hitching posts, simulating a small Negro jockey, popular as a driveway decoration.

*Lawn-jockey*

Miss O'Connor says she is interested in writing about people who have a spiritual life. Her interest derives from her own strong religious feelings. She is a Roman Catholic and she says that the old man in *The Violent Bear It Away,* dying after a life as itinerant pracher, echoes her convictions about religion. Her hero in this novel is young Tarwater, whom the elder man has reared as his successor.

Translations of *The Violent Bear It Away* are being prepared in Italian and Greek. It has been published in France as *La Sagesse dans la Sang* and in England under its American title.

Asked about work in progress, Miss O'Connor replies that she's "writing." A year ago, in Atlanta, she spoke of a volume of short stories she planned. "Sometimes what seems to be a short story proves to be something else when it's put down on paper."

Miss O'Connor lately acquired a handsome pair of tall bookcases in Savannah. They had belonged to members of her family. They are filled with the books she reads in the 1820 O'Connor home. Which led to her being asked what were her literary influences.

"Sometimes the most profound books are not the ones that bestir you most. Many years ago I read a volume of *The Humorous Stories of Edgar Allan Poe,* and I think that started me thinking of a writing career. Though, in fact, I began writing before I began reading. . . . And I'm sure Gogol influenced me."

Born in Savannah, Miss O'Connor lived there until she was 12. In 1940 she lived six months in Atlanta. Later she lived in New York and Connecticut, and she received her masters in fine arts at the University of Iowa, where she started her professional life. She is an only child. Mrs. Regina Cline O'Connor's empathy with her daughter is patent.

The daughter dedicated her first novel (now being republished) "To Regina."

# King of the Birds
Richard P. Frisbie/1962

From *Plymouth Traveler*, 3 (August-September 1962), 16-17. ©
1962 Chrysler Corporation.

When a peacock spreads his famous feathers, you get a double whammy from a hundred blazing "eyes." The effect has entranced people at least as far back as Solomon. In ancient times the birds were transported from southeast Asia to all parts of the known world as part of storied cargoes of "gold and silver, ivory, apes and peacocks."

Like their relatives, chickens and pheasants, peafowl are edible. The Romans considered them a delicacy roasted in their feathers. But in our country today peacocks, accompanied by their consorts, peahens, serve chiefly to beautify parks and country estates like the 1700-acre plantation of Flannery O'Connor at Milledgeville, Ga. Miss O'Connor, novelist and short story writer, has surrounded herself with 40 peafowl.

Peacocks aren't affectionate pets. They devote their energies to their own interests, eating and taking care of their trains. (The peacock's "tail" actually isn't a tail; the long feathers grow out of his back.) The peacock, a long-lived bird, does not acquire his train until his third year. Then he furls and unfurls it, screams when it's stepped upon and arches it carefully when he walks through a puddle.

During the spring and summer he struts for several hours each morning and evening, resting during the heat of the day. He usually performs at the same location, so that any peahen who secretly admires him will know where to find him. Secret admiration seems to be the rule among peahens. Flannery says, "If I have found anyone indifferent to the peacock's display, it is the peahen. She seldom casts an eye at it, but goes on about her business, diligently searching the ground as if any bug in the grass were of more importance."

When a peacock's train is spread wide, he tends to turn his back

95

on you. Then there's nothing to do but wait until he decides to turn around. The peacock is perverse. Flannery complains, "I have never known a strutting peacock to budge a fraction of an inch for truck or tractor or automobile. It is up to the vehicle to get out of the way."

The peacock grows as big as a turkey and the feathers of his train are five times as long as his body.

Peafowl eat snails, frogs, insects, grain, juicy grasses, bulbs and Flannery O'Connor's flowers. "Peacocks not only eat flowers; they eat them systematically, beginning at the head of a row and going down it. If they are not hungry, they will pick the flower anyway and let it drop. For general eating, they prefer chrysanthemums and roses."

When hatched, the young peacocks show little promise of the splendid raiment to which their princely heritage someday will entitle them. They are hard to raise because of the changeable weather of our temperate zone climate, but in the flock at Milledgeville many of the young survive each year. After the first winter their health tends to be good. One of the most arrogant of the O'Connor peacocks is "Limpy," who has been strutting with one foot for several years since refusing to yield the right of way to a mowing machine.

Peacocks are not entirely a luxury. At least one Florida citrus grower uses peacocks to eat insect pests in his orange groves. For Flannery, owning a king-size flock of the kingly birds involves many indirect expenses.

"The peacock likes to sit on gates or fenceposts and allow his tail to hang down. A peacock on a fencepost is a superb sight. Six or seven peacocks on a gate is beyond description, but it is not very good for the gate. Our fenceposts tend to lean and all our gates open diagonally."

# An Interview with Flannery O'Connor

## Gerard E. Sherry/Spring 1963

From *The Critic*, 21 (June-July 1963), 29-31. Reprinted by permission of Gerard E. Sherry.

**Sherry:** As a writer, do you feel it necessary to read and be aware of other contemporary writers?

**O'Connor:** It was necessary when I first began to write. Now it does not seem so necessary.

**Sherry:** Some suggest that the European novelists are over-rated and that we Americans produce the better breed. What is your view of this?

**O'Connor:** It sounds right to me, though I don't know enough about the new European novels to deserve an opinion. I do think the American novel is much more interesting than the British novel.

**Sherry:** Do you see any signs of a chance of fiction evolving new forms?

**O'Connor:** I wouldn't know about literary questions like that. So-called experimental fiction always bores me. If it looks peculiar I don't read it.

**Sherry:** Is the most valid function of fiction simply the recounting of a good story?

**O'Connor:** It depends on what you mean by "good" story. I take it a good story would be one which continues to rattle on at a great rate at the same time that it reaches a profound level of meaning. The novel is pretty much an individual affair and I guess the answer to this will differ with what the individual writer wants to do. I'm a very traditional sort of writer and I'm content to try to tell a good story as I've just defined it.

**Sherry:** Fiction writers have often used their stories as vehicles for making their audiences aware of and sympathetic with the author's main interests. Your work expresses a Christian outlook on life—do you deliberately set out to present such a view?

97

**O'Connor:** I think the view comes of itself, but I deliberately set out to make it work as a legitimate piece of fiction.

**Sherry:** If you would agree the artist's philosophy will unavoidably show through and as your characters are so often described as despairing, would you agree they reflect your view of Christianity?

**O'Connor:** My characters are described as despairing only by superficial critics. Very few of my characters despair and those who do, don't reflect my views. You have to get the writer's view by looking at the novel as a whole.

**Sherry:** What do you think is stifling the Catholic writer of today—that is, apart from the spectre of poverty?

**O'Connor:** I think it's the lack of a large intelligent reading audience which believes Christ is God.

**Sherry:** You live in a region where your family roots lie deep. This surely gives you a sense of stability, lacking in many fellow Americans. Has it had any meaning for you as a writer?

**O'Connor:** Yes, I'm sure it has. I'm not out to battle the world or reform it. I'm pleased to be a member of my particular family and to live in Baldwin County in the sovereign State of Georgia, and to see what I can see from here. Where I am seems to me a great base for the imagination.

**Sherry:** "There are many Souths," says Ralph McGill. Are the people of your rural South to be found in many of its far flung regions?

**O'Connor:** I've never lived anywhere in the South but Georgia, but the southerners I've met from elsewhere in the South are not confusable with northerners or westerners. However, my characters are not sociological types. I write "tales" in the sense Hawthorne wrote tales—though I hope with less reliance on allegory. I'm interested in the old Adam. He just talks southern because I do.

**Sherry:** The South is changing, we hear at every hand. Are the rural people we know through your stories vanishing?

**O'Connor:** No, they are just moving to the city. Southern cities are full of country people.

**Sherry:** Do Catholics living as such a minority in your town develop a self-consciousness or defensiveness or any other traits in common?

**O'Connor:** No. The Catholics in Milledgeville have always been

valuable in the community, and more or less indistinguishable from
their neighbors.

**Sherry:** Recently you wrote that if fiction is going to be taught in
the high schools, it should be taught as a subject and as a subject
with a history. What did you mean by this?

**O'Connor:** Well, I meant it as a corrective to the hit and run
methods of teaching it now. A friend of mine called me up not long
ago and asked if I could recommend a book of Faulkner's for her boy
in the eighth grade to read. He had a reading list—Faulkner,
Hemingway, Steinbeck, Warren and people like that, and for some
unexplainable reason, Irving Stone. He was supposed to read any
novels of theirs that he wanted to. Now, in my opinion, that's not fare
for the eighth grade. It takes experience to read modern fiction,
literary experience and moral experience both, and they don't have it
at that age and stage. I'd have them reading the great novels of the
nineteenth century.

**Sherry:** Do you think our high school English teachers are
confusing literature with social studies?

**O'Connor:** I know a good many who do. I would not be prepared
to say more than that.

**Sherry:** You seem convinced the student should have few rights in
relation to his educational formation. I recall your stating that the
student's taste should not be consulted, it should be formed. Can you
enlarge on this?

**O'Connor:** Well, I was talking strictly about literature courses. It
seems self-evident to me that the student is there to be taught what
there is to teach, not to be asked what he would like to learn or read.
I went to a "progressive" high school myself. I read what I wanted to.
Consequently, I read practically nothing. Reading was tolerated at
that school. I don't recollect that it was encouraged. I remember
reading a book of Ludwig Bemelman's about the hotel business. Or
maybe it wasn't by him. It was by somebody who ran the Algonquin.
That's bad. Not to be able to remember who wrote the book you
read in high school. The subjects were integrated with each other and
everything was a blur. About all I remember of those four years is the
way the halls smelled and bringing my accordion sometimes to play
for the "devotional." I'm sure the schools are better now, and it is

probably better to read Faulkner in the eighth grade than nothing. At the same time, it seems sort of insulting to Faulkner.

**Sherry:** Do you think we are doing anything to produce an élite of American Catholic writers similar to that of England or Ireland?

**O'Connor:** I think the only thing we can do is prepare readers for them and I think that is probably getting done slowly. I've been very impressed with the Catholic colleges I've visited in recent years. It takes more than the college, of course. It needs to start with the Sunday sermon and the literature in the back of the church.

**Sherry:** Let's take the Sunday sermon. Where do you think the pulpit is failing as a medium of instruction?

**O'Connor:** Of course, the purpose of the pulpit is to instruct in religion and to inspire the congregation to love God, not to assist it to be cultured, but it is doubtful how much religious instruction or inspiration can be got out of abstractions coupled with secondhand emotion and all the clichés in the book. I am in no position to say what the general level of preaching is today in the Church. You can't expect every priest to sound like Newman, but you can expect to feel that the sermon is fresh and that it has at least passed through the head and heart of the preacher recently. I should think that if you hear good sermons on Sunday, you would be more likely to recognize genuine sentiment if you met it in a novel or story or poem. Of course, you can't really say how these things work. I have a connection who married a Baptist. I don't know how much of a Baptist he was, but enough so that he didn't think the Catholic Church had much to offer. He went with her to Mass on Sundays though, and after he had been doing that about twelve years or so, he came into the Church. We were considerably surprised. I said to him, "Whatever got you interested?" and he said, "Well, the sermons were so terrible, I knew there must be something else to it to get all those people there Sunday after Sunday." The Lord can use anything, but you just think He shouldn't have to.

**Sherry:** Are you serious about the literature in the back of the church? I understand it consists mainly of Catholic pamphlets with little if any literary style.

**O'Connor:** Cast your eye over one of those racks and you get the impression that Madison Avenue has moved in and settled down, and judging from the ones I've seen the style runs from little-if-any to pure-bad. I'm not against pamphlets, but there's no reason why instructions should be badly written or lack style on principle. Sheed and Ward had a series of pamphlet-size books, the contents of which were taken from very good books on their particular subjects. They might be too expensive for the back of the church, but there's no reason that principle could not be followed with cheaper pamphlets. You understand, I have not read many of these pamphlets, and there may be plenty of good ones already. The point is they ought to be good. The church ought to have great respect for the written word wherever it is found, but particularly when it is found in the church.

**Sherry:** Does the Catholic press stimulate enough reading of books?

**O'Connor:** I don't have any way of knowing how many of them have good book pages, but I would just suspect that with the majority of them the book page gets short shift.

**Sherry:** What do you think the Catholic press can do to stimulate not only good reading, but good writing? Do you think there is enough good writing in the present day Catholic press?

**O'Connor:** I'm in no position to make general statements about the Catholic press, but there is enough of it so that anybody should be able to get what suits him. I receive the *Boston Pilot* and the *Davenport Messenger* and *The Georgia Bulletin* and the Operation Understanding Edition of the *Sunday Visitor.* That's enough Catholic papers to kill anybody, but I have reason for being interested in each. The writing in them is all right. It does not call undue attention to itself. I do think a paper ought to let you know where good writing can be found elsewhere. Now, the *Davenport Messenger* reprints a lot of good addresses and such, and I like that, and think Catholic papers ought to do more of that sort of thing generally.

**Sherry:** Do we have too many Catholic newspapers and magazines? Do you think we should have only first-rate national ones?

**O'Connor:** I suppose each one that is no good is one too many, but I don't think we should have only national ones. I think the paper should reflect the people of the region it serves. When *The Georgia Bulletin* starts sounding as if it were issued in Philadelphia, I'm going to drop my subscription.

**Sherry:** What about the oft-discussed Catholic daily?

**O'Connor:** It would have to be mighty good to survive, and I should think the odds were against that.

**Sherry:** Well then, do you believe Catholic criticism in relation to the arts has matured?

**O'Connor:** So much so that it is in danger of going off the other end. I get disturbed when I read articles that imply that the novel is about how man feels and that this is something belief doesn't enter into. The novelist does more than just find a symbol for feeling. Good fiction involves the whole range of human judgment.

**Sherry:** What do you think integration is doing to the culture of your native South?

**O'Connor:** I don't think it's doing anything to it. White people and colored people are used to milling around together in the South, and this integration only means that they are going to be milling around together in a few more places. No basic attitudes are being changed. Industrialization is what changes the culture of the South, not integration.

**Sherry:** Do you think that the philosophy of gradualism in relation to integration is the best one for the present situation?

**O'Connor:** What's best is what's possible. The word gradualism is just an abstraction which hides the concrete problem. If you mean by it that you integrate the libraries before you close the swimming pools, yes, that's best.

**Sherry:** How do southern manners bear on the racial turmoil?

**O'Connor:** Manners are the next best thing to Christian charity. I don't know how much pure unadulterated Christian charity can be mustered in the South, but I have confidence that the manners of both races will show through in the long run.

**Sherry:** What is your advice to the budding novelist?

**O'Connor:** I avoid giving him any when I can. Then I think it depends pretty much on the individual. You can always tell him to go somewhere and read.

# Flannery O'Connor: An Interview
## C. Ross Mullins, Jr./1963

From *Jubilee*, 11 (June 1963), 32-35. © 1963 *Jubilee*.

**Q.** What are your main concerns as a writer?

**A.** Well, when you write fiction, you both reveal and obscure the things you know best or feel most concerned about and I think that's the way it ought to be. I will admit to certain preoccupations that I get, I suppose, because I'm a Catholic; preoccupations with belief and with death and grace and the devil. If I'm less reticent than I ought to be about declaring these, it's because they haven't been recognized except by those who share them and sometimes not them. These preoccupations have to work themselves out by way of situations possible in the South, of course, and this creates confusion, as most readers rely on various critical clichés to explain Southern literature that don't explain anything.

**Q.** Why are Southern writers so good?

**A.** The South is a story-telling section. The Southerner knows he can do more justice to reality by telling a story than he can by discussing problems or proposing abstractions. We live in a complex region and you have to tell stories if you want to be anyway truthful about it.

**Q.** What about the grotesque in your work? Has it anything to do with your being a Southerner and the relations between people in the South, especially between Negroes and whites?

**A.** We're all grotesque and I don't think the Southerner is any more grotesque than anyone else; but his social situation demands more of him than that elsewhere in this country. It requires considerable grace for two races to live together, particularly when the population is divided about fifty-fifty between them and when they have our particular history. It can't be done without a code of manners based on mutual charity. I remember a sentence from an

essay of Marshall McLuhan's. I forget the exact words but the gist of it
was, as I recollect it, that after the Civil War, formality became a
condition of survival. This doesn't seem to me any less true today.
Formality preserves that individual privacy which everybody needs
and, in these times, is always in danger of losing. It's particularly
necessary to have in order to protect the rights of both races. When
you have a code of manners based on charity, then when the charity
fails—as it is going to do constantly—you've got those manners there
to preserve each race from small intrusions upon the other. The
uneducated Southern Negro is not the clown he's made out to be.
He's a man of very elaborate manners and great formality which he
uses superbly for his own protection and to insure his own privacy.
All this may not be ideal, but the Southerner has enough sense not to
ask for the ideal but only for the possible, the workable. The South
has survived in the past because its manners, however lopsided or
inadequate they may have been, provided enough social discipline to
hold us together and give us an identity. Now those old manners are
obsolete, but the new manners will have to be based on what was
best in the old ones—in their real basis of charity and necessity. In
practice, the Southerner seldom underestimates his own capacity for
evil. For the rest of the country, the race problem is settled when the
Negro has his rights, but for the Southerner, whether he's white or
colored, that's only the beginning. The South has to evolve a way of
life in which the two races can live together with mutual
forebearance. You don't form a committee to do this or pass a
resolution; both races have to work it out the hard way. In parts of the
South these new manners are evolving in a very satisfactory way, but
good manners seldom make the papers.

**Q.** How often do they make novels?

**A.** They have to be pretty stable before they make novels, that is to
say, good novels.

**Q.** You mentioned that you think of yourself primarily as a storyteller. That means you have to understand your audience. How does
this temper your work?

**A.** Well, I tell stories that frequently hinge on the things of belief,
and the man of our times is certainly not a believer. When I write a
novel in which the central action is baptism, I have to assume that for
the general reader, or the general run of readers, baptism is a

meaningless rite, and I have to arrange the action so that this baptism carries enough awe and terror to jar the reader into some kind of emotional recognition of its significance. I have to make him feel, viscerally if no other way, that something is going on here that counts. Distortion is an instrument in this case; exaggeration has a purpose.

**Q.** But you have plenty of readers who do believe—possibly more than who don't.

**A.** Well, this isn't a distortion or an exaggeration that destroys. The believer ought to know what's going on. I find that some of my best readers are Sisters. I spent two days at Marillac College, a seminary for the Daughters of Charity. The student Sisters told me that they understood Tarwater because they had had the same experience he had. It was a matter of vocation. That's all the understanding you could ask for.

**Q.** It's felt by some that religion and faith have been undermined in our age. Do you, as a Catholic writer, feel a moral responsibility to oppose this tendency through your writing?

**A.** I don't feel any moral responsibility to do this as a Catholic writer, no; but I won't say I don't get considerable glee out of doing it when it just happens that way. I think there is a danger in talking about the Catholic writer as if his religion blotted out or stood in opposition to his personality. The notion that Catholic writers are not free comes about by thinking that being a Catholic is something imposed from the outside against one's true feelings. You are a Catholic writer because you accept what the Church teaches, not because the Church is a vise in which you are caught.

I don't like the idea some people have that the novelist has this untouchable sensibility that ought to be left to its pleasure. What makes the sensibility good is wrestling with what is higher than itself and outside it. It ought to be a good bone-crunching battle. The sensibility will come out of it marked forever but a winner. What ails a lot of people is that the writer's so-called sensibility has had nothing to struggle with, no opposition. Conversely, in the case of some novels by Catholics, the writer's belief has had nothing to struggle with. Just as bad a situation.

**Q** Do you think there is, or can be, such a thing as the Catholic novel? Some people say the novelist shows us how man feels and that this is beyond distinctions of belief.

**A.** I think the novelist does more than just show us how a man feels. I think he also makes a judgment on the value of that feeling. It may not be an overt judgment. Probably it will be sunk in the work but it is there because, in the good novel, judgment is not separated from vision. I have a talk I sometimes give called "The Catholic Novelist in the Protestant South" and I find that the title makes a lot of people in the schools nervous. Why bring up such a distinction? Particularly when the word Christian ought to settle both. They think I'm going to kick up a lot of sixteenth-century dust, I guess. Actually what the Protestant South gives the Catholic novelist is something very good that he doesn't get elsewhere. Judgment is just as much a matter of relishing as condemning. The distinctions between Catholic and Protestant are distinctions within the same family, but every distinction is important to the novelist. Distinctions of belief create distinctions of habit, distinctions of habit make for distinctions of feeling. You don't believe on one side of your head and feel on the other.

**Q.** What about the novel today, do you think it's dead, dying, ailing or what?

**A.** The health of the novel is one thing that just doesn't interest me a bit. That's for English teachers to talk about.

**Q.** Are you working on another novel? Short story?

**A.** I'm working on a longish piece of fiction that I hope will turn out to be a novel but it never does to be sure. I'm not far enough along to know what'll happen with it.

**Q.** Have you enough stories for a second collection?

**A.** I suppose I do, but I'd prefer to have enough to select from and leave some out. Publishing a book is not my favorite sport; it's a necessary evil but I put it off as long as possible.

**Q.** Which do you like writing better, novels or stories?

**A.** Stories, because you know you've got something sooner. I might work on a novel several years before I was really sure I had a novel to work on. That's mighty tiresome.

**Q.** How does a story come into being? Do you create it or does it create you? Do you think there's a danger of a writer's exhausting his material?

**A.** I don't know that I could really say how a story comes into being. I suppose it's about fifty-fifty as to whether you create it or it creates you. If it's a good story, it's as much a revelation to you as it is to the reader. I'm afraid it is possible to exhaust your material. What you exhaust are those things that you are capable of bringing alive. I mean if you've done it once, you don't want to do the same thing over. The longer you write the more conscious you are of what you can and cannot make live. What you have to do is try to deepen your penetration of these things.

**Q.** By what standards do you judge your own work? Is objectivity difficult? Are you ever fully satisfied with a finished work?

**A.** I suppose the standards are largely instinctive. I have a sort of feeling for what I'm doing, else I wouldn't be doing it. I don't suppose objectivity is difficult. I wouldn't be attached to a sorry story just because I had written it. Sometimes you need time between you and the story before you can really see it whole; usually it's good to see how somebody else reads it. Distance is always a help. Sometimes I'm fully satisfied with something I've written but most of the time I'm just satisfied that this is the best I can do with my limitations.

**Q.** You once wrote that the creative action of the Christian's life is to prepare his death in Christ. How does this relate to your work as a writer?

**A.** I'm a born Catholic and death has always been brother to my imagination. I can't imagine a story that doesn't properly end in it or in its foreshadowings.

# Southern Writers are Stuck with the South
## Atlanta Magazine/1963

From *Atlanta Magazine*, 3 (August 1963), 26, 60, 63. © 1963
Communications Channels Inc. Reprinted by permission.

"Southern writers are stuck with the South and it's a good thing to be stuck with," says Flannery O'Connor.

The Georgia author of two novels and dozens of short stories, Miss O'Connor is the natural heir of the generation that produced what Yankee critics like to call "the Southern literary renaissance." With a magnificent comic gift and a profound sense of mystery, she still probes that blazing and tortured land which has been the province of Southern writers for four decades.

At Andalusia, a rambling white farm house near Milledgeville, Miss O'Connor is at work on a third novel whose title was suggested by the weekly advertisements of a ranting fundamentalist in the Atlanta newspapers. The dairy pastures are green now; the heat lies in a thin haze over the hills, sapphire feathered peacocks roost in the trees and the neighbors chat in wicker rockers on the front porch at evening. Yet the thirty-eight-year-old-writer, with the candid eyes and school girl face is well aware of the dramatic changes in the South.

The airless and exotic hothouses of Truman Capote and Tennessee Williams have been shattered by the Industrial Revolution, she points out, and the sleepy hamlets of the Agrarians are now bustling branch office towns. The wool hat politicians of Erskine Caldwell died with the county unit system. In Faulkner's only half mythical Yoknapatawha County, integration is at least proceeding with "all deliberate speed." And even the wild-eyed prophet-freaks of the O'Connor novels, *Wise Blood* and *The Violent Bear It Away*, have been replaced by beaming luncheon-club clerics.

"But the South had a distinctive character even before the Revolutionary War," says Flannery O'Connor. "As its history went on to be a history of defeat and as it has been in many respects the outcast of the nation since, its unity of feeling has held fairly firm, even though conditions are constantly changing."

Born in Savannah of an old Georgia family, she believes that "Southern history has reinforced what the fiction writer, who is any good, always has to show the world . . . that the human situation is a good deal more complex and cross-purposed than ideals and abstractions allow for. This is not unique, it's a function of art, but the South knows it better than the rest of the country."

"The best American writing has always been regional," says Flannery O'Connor. "But to be regional in the best sense you have to see beyond the region. For example, the Fugitives at Vanderbilt in the '20's felt that the South they knew was passing away and they wanted to get it down before it went, but they had a larger vision than just the South. They were against what they saw coming, against the social planner, fellow traveller spirit that came along in the next ten years. They looked to past and future to make a judgement in their own times."

Will today's social crisis produce a new literature? "To suggest such is, I think, to romanticize the race business to a ridiculous degree and to exaggerate out of all proportion the importance of the present crisis for literature," says the writer.

"The Negro will in the matter of a few years have his constitutional rights and we will all then see that the business of getting along with each other is much the same as it has always been, even though new manners are called for. The fiction writer is interested in individuals, not races; he knows that good and evil are not apportioned along racial lines and when he deals with topical matters, if he is any good, he sees the long run through the short run."

Referring to James Baldwin's recent and best selling outcry, *The Fire Next Time,* she grants that "the Southern Negro has a great deal to contribute to the literature of the South, but I think it will take a while for him to do this; when he does, I doubt it will be much like Baldwin's. I should expect it to be a great deal better."

As unique as "the presence of two races" is the fact that the South "is a real Bible Belt," says Miss O'Connor. "We have a sense of the absolute . . . a sense of Moses' face as he pulverized the idols." Signs of a prophetic Biblical fundamentalism still abound on the highways around Milledgeville—warnings of eternal damnation, exhortations to repent, assurances that "Jesus Saves." The Bible Belt influence is no less apparent in Southern literature.

"It gives us a kind of skepticism under God, a refusal to put relative things in the place of the Absolute," says Miss O'Connor. "It keeps our vision concrete and it forms a sacred heroic background to which we can compare and refer our own actions."

"I see from the standpoint of Christian orthodoxy," she has said. "For me the meaning of life is centered in our Redemption by Christ and what I see in the world I see in its relation to that . . . Writers who see by the light of their Christian faith will have, in these times, the sharpest eyes for the grotesque, for the perverse, for the unacceptable. The novelist with Christian concerns will find in modern life distortions which are repugnant to him and his problems will be to make these appear as distortions to an audience which is seeing them as natural."

Her magnificent demon-ridden prophets, raving in an Old Testament world devoid of Grace, "are images of man forced out to meet the extremes of his own nature," explains the writer. She grants that they may be a vanishing breed, but it is important that the new writers not lose the sense of mystery and evil which bred them. Southern writers may write about men in grey flannel suits, but they must not fail "to see that these gentlemen are even greater freaks than what we are writing about now," she says wryly.

The regional aspects of her fiction are bizarre and beguiling and they have been elaborately used by exuberant parodists who regard Miss O'Connor's tales as a sort of clever trick. But she avoids—and she advises others to avoid—"using all this regional matter simply to illustrate the region."

"The Georgia writer's true country is not Georgia, but Georgia is an entrance to it for him," says Flannery O'Connor. "One uses the region in order to suggest what transcends it," and her own unflinching gaze extends beyond problems and paraphernalia to "that realm of mystery which is the concern of prophets."

Readers who miss this point seldom get beyond the regional grotesqueries of Miss O'Connor's work—a fact she seems to understand and accept as serenely as she does the painful disease which has crippled her since girlhood.

# My Flannery O'Connor
Betsy Fancher/1975

From *Brown's Guide to Georgia*, 3 (March/April 1975), 16-22. ©
1975 Brown's Guide to Georgia.

Long before her death at the age of thirty-eight, Flannery O'Connor
had outgrown her early fame as the *enfant terrible* of Southern letters
and had won her place in history as a writer who probed, in a
distinctly Southern idiom, the mysterious outer reaches of reality that
are the province of the prophet and the poet.

"Southern writers are stuck with the South, and it's a good thing to
be stuck with," she once said to me and her two novels, *Wise Blood*
and *The Violent Bear It Away,* and her short stories are regional in
focus. But she had a horror of being known as a "Southern writer"
with all that entailed—the dialect stories, the moonlight and magnolia
myth, and the "hot house" school. "The woods are full of regional
writers and it is the horror of *every* serious Southern writer that he
will become one," she said.

Yet she knew that all good writing begins at home, that the best
American literature is regional, and that the smallest history can be
read in a universal light. "You know what's the matter with them?
They're not *frum* anywhere," she said of that slick new breed of
writers who have taken over the paperback book stalls. Flannery was
*frum* Georgia, and rather fiercely so; she once observed wryly in print
that the so-called anguish of the Southern writer derived not from the
fact that he was alienated from the rest of the country but that he was
not alienated enough. She gloried in the eccentricities of the region,
in the complications and contradictions with which it abounds, and
she found in Georgia a "collection of goods and evils which are
intensely stimulating to the imagination."

She was born in Savannah, grew up in Milledgeville, attended the
Woman's College of Georgia, and, except for a stint at Iowa State
and a brief apprenticeship in New York, she did most of her writing at

Andalusia, the 150-year-old Milledgeville farmhouse where she lived
with her mother, Regina. One can see it now, just off the highway, a
narrow, steeply roofed white farmhouse beside a tall white water
tank. Dairy cattle still graze the broad pastures in the shadow of the
blue hills.

It was here I first met her. My volume of short stories, *Blue River,*
had been published about the time of her first short stories, *A Good
Man is Hard to Find,* and my beloved English prof at Wesleyan, Dr.
George Gignilliat, drove me down to Milledgeville, where we sat in
comfortable rockers on her wide front porch and talked, watching the
peacocks she was so fond of preening themselves on the lawn. I
remember that even at that first meeting we laughed a lot for
Flannery and I had a similar sense of the ridiculous and always
giggled like school girls when we were together.

She told me that at the age of six she had appeared with her pet
rooster on the *Pathe News* and swore that was the pinnacle of her
career, though in her lifetime she was accorded almost every
accolade that can accrue to a short story writer in this country—three
O. Henry Memorial Awards, two *Kenyon Review* fellowships and two
national grants.

"If my characters speak Southern, it's because I do," she always
said, but it went a lot deeper than that. When The Misfit in "A Good
Man Is Hard to Find," after murdering a family of five on the
highway, says, "Jesus thrown everything off balance," he is doing
more than using dialect—he is going to the very heart of the Christian
mystery. Our history, customs, vices, and virtues are inherent in our
idiom, she said, and she was a master of the idiom. Impious but
devout, scathingly honest yet compassionate, deadly serious but
relentlessly comic, Flannery O'Connor was uniquely fitted to portray
the regional character, with its deep ambiguities, Gothic violence, wry
wit, and idiosyncrasies. If her characters often emerged as displaced
persons, it was because she felt that all human beings are displaced
persons standing in need of divine grace. If they were also freaks, she
took pride in being able to recognize a freak in a day when the man
in the grey flannel suit is celebrated as normal. Her prophet freaks,
she explained, were "figures of our essential displacement, images of
man forced out to meet the extremes of his own nature." Her
distortions and exaggerations were quite deliberate. To a twentieth-

century audience, reeling from the myths of Madison Avenue, she found it necessary to make her vision appear shocking. "To the hard of hearing you shout and to the almost blind you draw large and startling figures," she told me.

But she also understood that it is impossible to say anything about the mystery of personality "unless you put personality in the social context that belongs to it." She balked at the term "frame of reference," perhaps because so few of the critics really understood the nature of it. They thought it was the Southern landscape.

Socially, her context was the Bible Belt, and she had a penetrating eye for its grotesqueries—the tent revivals, the child evangelists, the sawdust salvations, and the high admonitions to "repent or burn in hell." She had no illusions about the South's being Christ-centered, but she found it "Christ-haunted." "Ghosts can be very fierce and instructive and they cast strange shadows," she once told me.

A Catholic, she said her faith in Christian doctrine furnished her with "a sense of continuity from Christ" and assured her a respect for mystery. It was this respect which safeguarded her from the pitfalls of regional writers who view the South only as a fertile scene of local color. In the sparest and most vivid prose, she used the region to suggest what transcended it. "The whole gaze," she said, "has to extend beyond the surface, beyond mere problems, until it touches that realm of mystery which is the concern of prophets."

Now that she is gone, she is lionized—the subject of more academic dissertations than any writer I know of and that would have amused her because of her innate sense of the absurdity of most master's theses. Most of the publicity she received in her lifetime—all the critical accolades and academic analyses—would have outraged her had she not had the saving grace of humor—a humor born I think, of a towering courage and the gracious habit of living with death from the blood disease which crippled her in her twenties and brought her back from New York to the farm where her regal, strong-willed mother could care for her and spare her any household duties so she could devote her energies to writing. The farm, she once told me, "is nothing to me. Once in a while I pick up an egg." But she loved the peacocks, and she kept a menagerie of exotic birds which she delighted in showing me, though I wince at feathery, flying things.

Her reputation was world-wide, but she was rooted in Georgia;

and crippled as she was, she often delegated me to accept a local award, making an appropriate speech of appreciation in her behalf. It was a chore which always required buying a hat—something she never knew; but most writers' groups were behatted ladies and I dutifully acquired the appropriate costume until my husband burst out laughing at my final acquisition—a wide-brimmed straw hat abloom with lemon lilies.

Flannery was a stern, conscientious and inspired critic of my own fiction, but she seriously chastised me only once—when I abandoned the short story and returned to journalism to help my widower husband start his law practice and raise his three small daughters. But she was living then under the spectre of death and I was coming alive, and much as she would dislike the expression, we were acting from an opposite "frame of reference."

The last accolade she received from her native state, an award from a writers' group, she accepted herself. It was held at the Atlanta Historical Society on Peachtree Street and she asked me to attend. I was then book editor of the *Atlanta Journal-Constitution*, but she didn't want any publicity. She had something unique to say—her last talk—and she wanted me to hear it because she said I was the only critic who really understood her work, perhaps because we both worked and lived from the same "point of reference," a belief in divine grace. Or maybe it was only because we could laugh together.

After her talk, rendered haltingly on crutches, we went out into the garden to spend what we both intuitively knew were our last moments together. We were alone, amid vivid camellias and great oaks, and there seemed so little time and so much to say, when our talk was interrupted by a stranger—a prophet freak, and Flannery, even in that last week of her life, couldn't resist a prophet freak, a young one with a taste for good books and literary ambitions, drunk as a lord, in the luminous, desperately articulate high point of a manic phase that was to hospitalize him the next day.

Flannery, thinking perhaps that we had already said it all, or given as much as we had to give to one another at that particular time, squandered those last moments of our life together listening with avid interest to the young prophet, taking notes with that fantastic intellect of hers on his rantings about literature and life and the divine, according him the profound respect which inspired madness deserves. A cab interrupted the conversation. The driver helped her up on her crutches and we parted, she knowing, I devoutly believe, that someday I would find in her last book her last message to me, and I assured by her final act of compassion to a mad stranger that she at last understood why I had abandoned literature for life.

# Index

## T

Taylor, Peter, 67
*Time,* xvii
Turner, Margaret, viii, xviii, 41–43

## U

*The Union Recorder* [Milledgeville], 3, 4
University of Iowa, 4, 6, 43, 55, 59
Updike, John, xiv, 17

## V

Vanderbilt University, xi, xv, 19–36

*Vagabond,* 19

## W

Warren, Robert Penn, xv, 19–36; *All the
    Kings's Men,* 22–23
Waugh, Evelyn, 89
Wells, Joel, viii, x, xi, xix, 85–90
Welty, Eudora, 7, 70
Wesleyan College, xv, xvi, 61
West, Anthony, xv
Williams, Tennessee, 7, 42, 86